Lillian,
Thank you for being a
blessing to me
my God continue
you.

TEN
YEARS
STRONG

TEN
YEARS
STRONG

The God of Miracles

DIANA STRICKLAND

XULON PRESS

Xulon Press
2301 Lucien Way #415
Maitland, FL 32751
407.339.4217
www.xulonpress.com

Unless otherwise indicated, Scripture quotations taken from the King James Version (KJV)–*public domain*.

This book Ten Years Strong is based on true events. The names have been changed to respect their privacy.

Printed in the United States of America.

ISBN-13: 978-1-54566-955-6

Thank You, Jesus!

I would like to thank my Heavenly Father for blessing me to write this book. I love you so much for believing in me, encouraging me, and faithfully loving me. Ten Years Strong is a celebration of life! Thank you, Jesus, for this journey that shall continue.

Amen

Table of Contents

CHAPTER ONE

Awakening

The year was 2005 when I sat in my bathtub, crying to Jesus. It was one of those quiet cries. The ones you have where no one but Jesus can hear. I was in my big empty townhouse, alone. My husband, Brandon and I decided to separate after only nine months of marriage. We were sleeping in two different parts of the house. He was downstairs sleeping on an air mattress in our living room area, while I was upstairs sleeping in our bedroom. We didn't have much furniture, just a bed with two TVs.

Brandon and I had conflicting work schedules. I worked during the day as a leasing consultant when he worked overnight at a distribution building. Brandon also attended classes at a university and served in the National Guard once a month. We never really saw each other however we found time to fight most of the time he was at home. The fights grew intense. The last fight was worse than the one before. I put my hands on him as he was heading to work. As I turned around to go upstairs, he placed his arms around my neck. He dang near choked me to death.

Our fights were filled with anger. You would think that we disliked and hated one another. He would scream, curse me out, including calling me a Bitch, and he barely took me out on dates. On his days off from work, he would either sleep or go out to the night clubs with his friends. I would return the disrespect by putting my hands on him, along with kicking

1

him out the townhouse monthly, also threaten to divorce him. Every so often, he would go to a hotel to spend the night. Other nights I would go to my jobs model apartments where I worked to rest. We were dysfunctional. We were out of control, with no self-control, nor any thoughts about how our actions were hurting the other person. There was pride involved, and we were both to blame.

However, there was a point where I suggested that we seek counsel. Brandon shut that down. He said that we didn't need it. I even went so far as to go to our local bookstore and purchased two books about marriage. We never read either book. Our sex life was the only thing that kept us together. After our last fight, I got a revelation that scared me. The revelation was that we would live our lives like this, so up and down and not together. We would continue to fight. We would continue to live in separate parts of the house. He would continue to not talk to me for weeks.

In my eyes, Brandon was content with his decision to not try to work this marriage out, and that scared me. I didn't like the position we were in. I was not comfortable with our living arrangements. I never thought that I would walk into my house, living with somebody, and they would totally check out on me. This hurt me to the core. In my mind, if we wouldn't fix it, then we needed to separate and live in different homes.

I had one thing on my mind the day I was sitting in our bathtub. I desired to give my life over to Jesus. I desperately desired to start my life completely over. I had nowhere else to turn. I had no idea how to fix my life. I kept trying it my way to be this "good person." This wasn't working out for me. God was the only option I had. I did it wrong for so long. I couldn't think of a better person to give my life to than Jesus. All of my decisions led me to God. I was tired. I had enough of my bad track record of failures. I had enough word and prayer deposited in me. I had been a lukewarm Christian, but this time I was serious.

That day in the bathtub, I surrendered my life to God with tears of pain and a broken heart. I went to sleep but when I woke up I had a made-up mind. I woke up stern on my decision. I called Brandon to have a meeting at home. We agreed that he would move out to find another place to live within thirty days. When I walked away, I had a sense of peace within me. I knew in my heart that we would be okay. Finally, I felt a heavy weight lifted off my shoulder. I made a decision and the plan was to not go back nor look back.

I talked to God and told Him that I wanted two things from Him. The first thing was that I didn't want anybody to have an opinion about my transformation. I wouldn't listen to anyone about how to dress like a Christian, what music to listen to, what shows to watch. I only wanted God to help me out. You see, in my past, I had tried to change my ways for God. I got too bored with this Christian lifestyle, so I fell right back into sin a lot worse than I was before. This time I wanted God to work on me from the inside out. I figured that He knew what He was doing and He would help me out, and I wanted to listen to Him and Him only. The other thing I talked to God about and that was a desire to not move out of the state of New Jersey unless He told me specifically that I had to move. I didn't care what others thought or said.

Brandon began to look for a new apartment. I went to the local grocery store to pick up an apartment guidebook. I left the book on the kitchen counter for him to look over. I had no idea what I was going to do. I had no worries or cares about that. I wasn't concerned. I had peace. Because I was able to transfer as a leasing consultant within the company in Property Management from Illinois to New Jersey. As part of the perks of being a leasing consultant you receive a discount off of your rent, usually fifty percent off yet even with my discount I knew our rent was more than I wanted to pay. I also believed that I should search for a new place as a fresh start in my life.

Shortly after it crossed my mind that I would have to find a new job paying more money, I received a phone call from a temp agency. To my surprise, the gentleman on the other line told me that I sent my resume to their company about six months back. I thought that was odd since I had no reason six months ago to send my resume. I just listened to him as he continued to explain this new position with a well-known real estate company that was paying twice as much as I was being paid as a leasing consultant. The temp agent shared with me that he believed I was the perfect match for this position. He went over my resume and was convinced that I was the perfect one for this opportunity. Before we hung up the telephone, we scheduled a meeting at a local restaurant. At our meeting he presented a great package deal during my lunch break. This position at this real estate company was a promotion into management. I would work from 9 am to 5 pm, with weekends off and holidays. I would get paid enough money to live and survive. I seized this opportunity that seemed to have landed on my lap. The temp agent set up an interview with the property manager and director of this real estate company. I answered all their questions perfectly and I was offered the position not long after the interview. It was as if this position was tailored specifically for me. All that I had learned in my previous years as a leasing consultant at other properties in other states equipped me for this perfect God-designed moment.

Olivia and her kids were bored with living in Maryland. She said that her children didn't care too much for the schools and they didn't like the state, so they were driving back to Illinois. On their way to Illinois, she asked me if I needed a car. She wanted to give me their new silver Nissan Altima. The only requirement I had was to send her the monthly car note and pay the car insurance. Her family dropped off the car for me. Just like that, I had two blessings, back to back.

Brandon was looking for an apartment. We agreed that the last day of the thirty days, he would be packed up and gone. It would hurt me to see him go. I preferred that he was gone by the time I got home from work. But he didn't disappoint in the drama department. He was still there in the townhouse the day I came home. We had a heated argument that included slamming doors and threatening to call the police.

I stormed out of the townhouse, and drove away, with the impression that he would be gone when I returned. I stayed away for about thirty minutes. As I was driving back in the direction of my home, I stopped at the red traffic light. Right across the street was Brandon in his truck at the gas station, getting gas. He was moving back home to New York.

God put it in my heart to begin to search for a new apartment. I got an apartment guidebook and began to circle the apartment communities I would be interested in visiting. I went to a few apartment communities but only went into one appointment. With the other ones, I was picky. They weren't my preference. One of the apartment communities had a dumpster right where I drove into the community. There were so many black crows that I missed my appointment and turned around and drove away.

The final apartment I drove to was about a thirty-minute straight shot from my new real estate job. This community was a mile away from the main road, right behind the DMV, but as I continued down the road I would come up to it behind trees. Like this community was secluded. I loved it when I laid my eyes on it. Within five minutes of me filling out the apartment application, the property manager said that I was approved. She walked me to my new apartment. I needed a key to get inside the building. My apartment was on the first floor with a balcony, wood floors, plenty of closet space and new appliances in the bathroom and kitchen. The apartment was new. I could smell the scent of newness. I was excited and very pleased with Jesus. He did all this for me. No way should I have been approved for such an apartment in Morris County with my jacked-up credit. With Jesus, all things are possible. God is our Savior. He blessed me with a new car, a new apartment, and a new job. WOW!

I figured since I was young, with spare time, I could work a second job. I grabbed the Yellow Pages phone book and proceeded to send my resume to hotels listed in nearby areas. Shortly after faxing my resume and calling random hotels to see if they were hiring, one of those hotels called me back to schedule an interview. It was right across the street from my new real estate job. The general manager and his assistant were astonished that they paid a lot of money to advertise for the overnight position when I found them in the Yellow Pages. I was offered an overnight position and began to work full-time at both jobs.

I was on the right path. God was moving very swiftly on my behalf. Although I didn't belong to a church, I waited for God to lead me in the right direction concerning my future church home. I took church membership very seriously. I was not the type to jump from one church to another. Wherever God would send me would be my church family. In the meantime, I went to Blockbuster to purchase movies, One Night with the King, King David, Moses, and JESUS. I was falling in love with God. We were building a solid relationship.

This relationship was easier to build than working with the women at my two jobs. The ladies at both jobs seemed to be guarded and not that welcoming to new people. I had a hard time even going to lunch with coworkers. Someone told me that most women on the East Coast only had friendships that went back to elementary school. It was like I had to go to school with them to be accepted. I learned quickly about developing a thick skin. The East Coast was very different than Birmingham Alabama where I was born and raised. It was a culture shock.

Down South from my eyes was more about family, friends, church, and home-cooked meals. While the East Coast was about the fast pace, working hard, making money, and wearing designer everything and having nice things. I was adapting fast to my surroundings.

I sometimes spoke to Brandon. We stayed in touch. Although he was frustrated about moving back home to his mother. I can honestly say that he was resilient. He took college courses online, worked full time, all while being in the reserves. He had a lot of determination when it came to working but in relationships, he struggled.

I just had to give the people on the East Coast some time to come around. In like two months, other people began visiting me at my cubicle. I was no longer eating by myself in my car. I was being invited to hang out, not only during lunch but to their house. I even made a friendship with one of the ladies from my hotel job, Sophia. She was a beautiful young lady with a bright future. She was also one of the supervisors for the second shift. She eventually became my personal alarm clock also. If I didn't show up for my shift on time to relieve her, within ten minutes she was calling my phone. Often times I would be running late because I overslept. I had an alarm clock that went off, but somehow I would turn it off and fall back to sleep. Half the time, I didn't even remember doing all this, but Sophia became my backup alarm clock. She never complained about it or made me feel bad about showing up to work thirty minutes late. You would think that she would hightail it out of the job after a long shift, but instead, she would stay to talk to me. I didn't have to apologize to her for being late. I did once, but she brushed it off. She was sweet as pie with a soft-toned voice. She had one problem that made her look bad. It was her choices in the men she made her boyfriend and the crowd of people she called friends. She had a boyfriend who had pretty green eyes. He was handsome to look at, but he was a problem. He would borrow her car, and drive around with his baby mother. In Sophia's car. He not only had his baby mother in the car but one time that we knew about, he let her drive Sophia's car. He drove her car into a ditch, which she only complained to me about. Ask me if anything changed? Nope! She let him and a couple of his friends rent a room on her discount. They got kicked out for smoking weed and for being loud. I tried to talk some sense into her, but before I could almost convince her, she moved on to the next bad boy who was equally bad as the last one.

I admired how non-judgmental she was. Always willing to extend a helping hand. Sophia became more than just a work friend. We hung out outside of the hotel also. She and

I would go to Morristown bars that transformed into dance floors at night. She and I would dance the night away, just laughing, showing out, and bar hopping. I had a thought that this club thing would eventually have to stop. I didn't have the heart to stop it at this moment, but I knew in my heart that this part of my life would have to come to an end sooner than later. When I wanted to go to Atlantic City, because I heard from coworkers at the real estate office that there was a lot of fun things to do, I asked Sophia if she would like to go. I asked her to drive us there and back since this wasn't her first time driving there. She was willing to drive us there, but she didn't have any money. I suggested that I would pay for our hotel, which we received on an employee discount. I offered to pay for half of the gas, but I would also pay for her food. She agreed with no payback and we headed to Atlantic City within two-weeks.

When we arrived in Atlantic City, we immediately went to our hotel room to unpack and take pictures. It was fall, so I wore a light pink sweater that had pretty prints on it. I wore the sweater over a dark pink sheer tank top. It didn't take us long to go walk on the Boardwalk and go to a really nice restaurant that had animal figurines displayed throughout it. We walked to the casino where we played on the slot machines. I mainly focused on the dime and nickel slots. I won back all the money I spent on Sophia for our trip. I thanked God for helping me to win back all the money.

When we were done with the casino, we were walking to her truck to go to the hotel when we passed Jay-Z's 40/40 nightclub. We looked at each other and decided to go in. We were both interested in finding out what all the hype was about. We walked around the club to scope out the scene before we hit the dance floor to cut a rug. We must've been on the dance floor, laughing it up and having a good time, dancing by ourselves, when a short man came to me to tell me that his friend wanted me to come to him. His friend was in a roped-off sitting area. I looked back at him. It looked like there was an entourage of many men with him. I turned back around and kept dancing and having a good time with Sophia. I brushed him off. But this guy was determined. After him coming to me to say the same thing four times, I decided to go see what this guy wanted. I was never a stranger in the club. It's always been a place to meet cool people while dancing. It's never been that serious type of place for me. I grabbed Sophia's hand and we followed this short guy to where his friend was sitting. I sat next to the man who called me. It was kind of dark in the club, so I do not remember what he looked like. I just remember there were a lot of men sitting with him and Sophia didn't have a place to sit, so one of the men grabbed her hand and told her that she could sit on his lap. The guy who I sat next to was trying to talk to me, but I was distracted as I glanced at Sophia.

Two of the men kept asking me if I knew who the guy I was talking to was. Someone from his clique told me to look him up online. His friends told me that he played a pro sport and was retired. I didn't know who he was, because, for one, it was dark inside, and two, I never was into pro anything, so it didn't matter to me. I was from down South, we didn't care much about that. I kept looking at Sophia when the young man continued to move his legs up and down while she was sitting on his lap. The man and a few other men I could see were laughing and trying to talk to her. She looked uncomfortable, which made me concerned. I excused myself, took Sophia by the hand, and we headed back to the dance floor.

The retired pro athlete followed me to the dance floor a few seconds after I left him, but he could tell that I wasn't interested, so he danced to one song and walked away. When Sophia and I were heading out of the nightclub, I glanced in the direction of the roped-off area and found out he was someone unique. There was a line of half-dressed women waiting to be in his presence. I smiled inside as we walked out, and headed back to the hotel to rest.

The next morning, we drove back to New Jersey. Sophia dropped me off at our hotel to get my car. I drove my car with a heavy foot, blasting the Mary Mary gospel album. I was speeding going 75 MPH in a 20 MPH speed limit on the main road. Just when I was about to turn the corner in the direction of my apartment, I was stopped by an unmarked police car that was off the road. I got the most expensive speed ticket, dang near $400. I made a payment arrangement with the courts to pay this ticket off. You had better believe that was the last time I had a heavy foot. I mainly drove within the speed limit. I also made a clear decision to never go back to the nightclub. I thought that the nightclub was the one thing that kept me from truly serving the Lord and following His commandments. The club was connected to my sin and I had to let it go and move on from this part of my life. I had to choose following the Lord.

Since Sophia and I didn't hang out in the club, which was the one thing that we shared in common, we lost interest in hanging out or talking on the telephone. We began to grow distant from one another. She left the hotel where we worked to work at a different company.

Falling More in Love with God

When I still worked as a leasing consultant I met this tall, dark-skinned, handsome man in a business suit who was looking for a townhouse. While giving him a tour of our community during our conversation I mentioned that I was going through a divorce. Chris asked for my cell phone number. I gave it to him not thinking much about that since I wasn't looking for anything romantic. I was okay with having new friends. I explained myself to Chris the first night we spoke over the telephone. I told him what the deal was. He seemed to understand, and he had just ended a serious relationship, so we had something in common, I thought. We talked without seeing each other for six months, then he made it clear to me that it was time for us to start hanging out. I really appreciated his patience. He knew that I was separated from my husband and I was not interested in rushing into anything else so fast. Also, I had my plate full of working two full-time jobs. I couldn't make time for myself, nor did I have time to entertain anyone else. However, I thought it was nice of him to wait so long just to have dinner with me without any pressure. He seemed to care and understand. He was also busy with his job, which allowed him to travel frequently, and which was another reason why we never met up. This seemed to work out for both of us. I began to give serious thought about going out with Chris. I wasn't ready to go out on dates with another man, but I thought, "What's the big deal?" We mostly talked on the telephone at night when I was at my evening job.

One evening I dropped my laundry off at the hotel where I worked, to get it dry cleaned. That was one of the perks of working my overnight shift. I received dry cleaning for free. When I was there, laughing it up with my co-workers, Chris called. I asked him if I could call him back when I left the hotel. He said yes, but he called me back in ten minutes. I thought that was strange, however, I brushed it off. A week later I was enjoying a movie at home, and it was coming to an end when Chris called. I told him that I was watching this good movie and I would call him right back when the movie ended. Chris must've called me back less than ten minutes after we hung up. I thought this was odd. Two times I told him that I would call him back, and both times he called me right back in like ten minutes from us hanging up the telephone. I didn't know what to make of this, but I thought that it was time for me to stop talking to Chris. I felt that he did something that immediately turned me off and made me not interested in talking to him anymore. I sent him a text that we should stop talking, that it wasn't him but me. But I appreciated his friendship. That night while I was taking a break at work. I received a missed call. There was a lady on my voicemail telling me about Chris being her fiancé. Chris had been lying to her, saying that I was their real estate agent. I sat there in disbelief, wondering if I should call her back, which

I eventually did. The call went to her answering machine. I left her a voice message to let her know that I was not their real estate agent and that Chris and I had been talking non-stop for six months.

I honestly couldn't believe that he didn't tell me about his fiancée. And where was she when I was talking to him on the phone for hours? I remembered that most of the time when I called him, he never picked up the telephone, but he called me right back. Things started to make sense and I knew that I missed those signs because I wasn't invested. Chris called me multiple times to try to explain himself to me, but I was not willing to listen. I had a made up mind to leave this joker alone.

All was well at both of my jobs. I was arriving to work at the hotel on time. Since Sophia was no longer my alarm clock. At my real estate job, I was like a star. I shined in every meeting that I was in with the clients. I knew the answer to every question even before they finished their thought. They were highly impressed. I was receiving praise from coworkers, clients, everyone.

My real estate company didn't require that I have my real estate license, but they encouraged it. I had tried to get my real estate license in two other states and failed the test in each one, so I thought why not try in New Jersey. I was always close to passing, surely the third try would be the charm. The closer that I got to Jesus, the better my thinking was. I knew in my heart that I didn't want to go back to my husband, yet we were still intimate. He was starting to come around more often, but only to visit. Whenever he would leave, I would watch from my bedroom window as he got into his truck, and wonder why he didn't ask to stay over. We were moving further and further apart.

Although Brandon and I were separated not yet divorced he kept contact with me even confiding in me. He shared with me how difficult it was to live with his mother. I suggested that he move back into the apartment community where he was living before he moved me from Illinois to New Jersey after we got married. When he moved me to New Jersey in his apartment I asked him to give his furniture to his mother so that we could start fresh and I persuaded him to move us out of his apartment and into the townhouse where I was working as a leasing consultant. Brandon never complained and agreed to everything but now that we were no longer together I thought it was best for him to move back to those same apartments where he was living before I arrived. Brandon agreed and not only did he get approved but he moved back within no time.

As I was falling more in love with God, I was cutting back and letting go of a lot of things. I loved ratchet reality TV but I knew the more I watched it and the cursing and sexual content, that it was not good for my spirit. So I stopped watching it. I even threw away CDs that went against my moral compass. It was hard for me to throw away those CDs because a lot of the music was my jam. I enjoyed a lot of the tracks for their beat and the artist. I also paid a lot of money on it. Instead of giving them away, I threw them away. It didn't make sense for me to give something away that I deemed distasteful. I also replaced the secular music with Christian artist music. When I went into the music store I purchased albums based on what the artists looked like on the cover. I knew who Fred Hammond, Kirk Franklin, Mary Mary, and Israel Houghton were, so I purchased their CDs, but with all the new artists, I purchased their albums based on how pretty they were on their album cover. To my surprise, the albums were good.

God began to change my speech. My coworker, Tiffany, worked the overnight shift with me, but at a different hotel location. We would sit on the telephone for hours, gossiping and talking about what guest she slept with that week. She was very sexual. She almost slept with every good looking man she checked in and I am being honest. She bragged about it to anyone who would listen. She cursed a lot and she was funny. The closer I was getting to God, I began to not like what I was hearing. I didn't know how to stop it, other than pretending like I was busy or that it was my nap time. She and I would sneak a few hours of sleep. I would take a pillow and blanket to make myself comfortable. I locked the hotel front door and dozed off to sleep for three hours. She would do the same, but this girl was a trooper. She brought in a rollaway bed and slept on that. We joked and laughed about how we behaved. It was terribly funny.

Some days I found myself getting angry and frustrated with people that I disagreed with. I would yell and then apologize to that person a million times and cry afterward. I found myself apologizing and getting emotional more often than I wanted. How I dressed even bothered me. I once sought attention from men by wearing tight and see-through clothing that now no longer pleased me. In fact, I became embarrassed, so I went to the clothing store to purchase a size bigger. You could say that I was a work-in-progress.

I was proud to be holding down two full-time jobs and now starting real estate classes again. I was impressed with God and how He was changing my life, and celebrated having relationships with other women. I had been working at my two jobs for a year, and that was a huge accomplishment, with no drama at work. It was all smooth sailing.

Santrese was one of the women I met at my real estate job. She was an employee for five years. We met after I celebrated a year of working there. Her department moved into our building. They were assigned to sit a few feet away from my cubicle. When I first met Santrese, she was walking around, chatting it up with almost everyone. She was popular and seemed really excited to be surrounded by her friends. She was in her mid-forties and outgoing. Her personality matched mine in that we both liked to be social. She talked a lot and I liked that about her. You wouldn't be able to guess her age by looking at her, for she had a young soul. When she came to work, she talked a lot about her boyfriend. He always called her and sent her flowers at work just because. I looked forward to the day when a man would send me flowers at work.

One day, she came to work not in the same spirit as many times before. We inquired why her mood changed. She shared with us that her man was cheating on her. When she confronted him, he had a lot of bad words to say. He became violent and he left their townhouse abruptly to move in with the other woman. On top of all the disrespect, after they had been together for five years, she found out that he did not pay the rent and their electricity was about to be shut off in a couple of days. She needed to move out quick. She asked her friends at work to help her move out. I decided to join the ladies. We all met at the townhouse she once shared with her ex-boyfriend. We all helped her move out of her things.

As we were lifting and moving, she confided that she had nowhere to go. She told me that she did not want to move in with her parents. I felt sorry for her current situation, so I told her that she could come and live with me for as long as she needed. I told her that I would give her a copy of my key so that she would be able to come in and out as she pleased. I told her that I was barely at home, so she would have peace of mind and relax. She hugged and thanked me. She was amazed that I would be so kind as to open my doors to her after only getting to know her for three months. I felt a peace in my spirit like this was the right thing to do. I was sympathetic to her situation. I told her someone should enjoy my furniture since I was barely there. She smiled and said thank you.

I went on to encourage her by letting her know that I was not expecting her to pay any money towards my rent or bills, not even food or toiletries. She offered but I rejected the idea of her paying me any amount of money. I told her that these things would have to be paid if she wasn't there. When she moved into my apartment she only brought a small bag of clothes and personal things and her air mattress. In the morning I woke up to exercise to Tae Bo and make a big bowl of salad. She and I went to her favorite restaurant, Red Lobster, which was down the street from my apartment. One time I brought her dinner from a guy who I met at my hotel job. He was in town for business. He offered to take me out to dinner but instead, I asked if he could get both Santrese and myself dinner which he did. I didn't hear back from him as he had other plans for me that I was not going to do. If you know what I mean?

Santrese was grateful for her experience at my home which motivated her to search for a new place and move out of my apartment after only being with me for less than three months. It was a new townhouse in a new development in Newark. I told her that she could take her time moving out of my place but she was encouraged and motivated to move out and on with her life. Secretly I was sad to see her leave. I enjoyed her company but I understood her desire to start her life fresh. She was moving in the right direction and I couldn't be happier for her. We became even closer and she continued to share how well I treated her at my place to others. I wished that she didn't tell everyone especially with me standing right beside her.

Just as Santrese was packing up to leave I grabbed a box out of my closet that was filled with papers. In the midst of these papers were some of my old poems that I had written years back. I wanted to read them to her to receive some kind of feedback. She sat back and listened to me as I kept reading. When I finished reading them to her she gave me positive feedback. The very next day I brought the poems to work. I read them to the other ladies at my real estate job and they all had similar responses as Santrese. This made me happy and encouraged me to continue to write more poems to publish a poetry book.

One night while at my hotel job, I was leaning back on a chair when my eyes spotted a piece of paper with a list of nearby churches. I was confused when I picked up this list because I never knew it existed for the entire year I was at this job. It was like it just appeared out of nowhere. I scanned through it to find that there was a church not far from my two jobs. I went to visit it on Sunday. As soon as I stepped foot inside this church building, I knew immediately this church was for me. It felt like home. My pastor was Italian and he spoke the word of God. He fed us bread from heaven. This church was nondenominational and come-as-you-are. They were very diverse with blacks, whites, Italians, Latinos, Africans, Asians, and Indians. I mean, people from all walks of life were attending this church. I came every Sunday to their second service, sometimes wearing a cap and jeans. I was glad to be in the building. I thanked God for blessing me with a church home.

I could not have planned a better life for myself, even though there were times of sorrow. Sometimes I missed the idea of being with Brandon, but in my heart, I made a decision to not look back and continue with the process of being separated with the ending result of a divorce. I was driving on the highway when I saw a billboard sign that said that you can get a divorce for less than $400.00. I reached out to Brandon who agreed to pay half of the fee. I drove about thirty minutes to a building where they assist you with filling out the divorce papers. The paperwork seemed to be the easy part.

Olivia called me to see if I wanted to go to a girl's vacation trip to Jamaica. She would arrange the entire trip with an agent to include travel and the resort. She told me that we would go to an all-inclusive resort. That was the first time I heard about all-inclusive with a beach, water, and live performance. "Sign me up," I told her. I started telling the ladies at my real estate job where we were planning to go. When I told them the part of Jamaica was Hedonism 111. They looked back at me with concerned eyes and asked me if I knew where I was going and what that meant. Of course, I didn't, so they asked me to look it up. When I looked up the resort online, I was taken aback. I called Olivia to confront her about our location. All she said was, "I should have known what that word meant." Yeah as if I go around saying words like that or know people who use that type of language. I couldn't believe her but I had it processed in my brain to go.

I had no fear and believed in my heart that this trip would be everything that I hoped for, pleasant, fun, and peaceful.

Olivia was bringing two girlfriends with her on this trip. I decided to ask Tiffany if she wanted to come, and just like me, she was all for it. Tiffany told me this was her first time on a vacation trip with a group of ladies. She had never been out of the country, so this was equally exciting for the both of us. I was glad that we were able to share this experience together. She and I grew closer together in the last couple of months. We had some disagreements, but I wanted us to continue to grow. We hung out a couple of times at the club together before I decided to quit the club scene. She drove to my apartment one evening when she was tired of driving. She slept in my bed while I slept on the couch. I found myself extending myself to people and making them feel warm and welcomed because God had blessed me exceedingly.

When I finished furnishing my dining room, I invited Tiffany to my apartment along with three other ladies for a nice dinner. Everyone was to bring a plate. Tiffany kept complaining about my homemade mac and cheese. This was the only dish I knew how to cook besides my smothered baked chicken, which I was so proud to introduce, but she just had to dis it. The other ladies who were at the dinner told me that Tiffany was a negative soul and that I should reconsider calling her my friend. I heard the ladies but Tiffany had a bad history. I knew a lot about Tiffany's past that caused me to have sympathy towards her. When she was much younger, she was sexually assaulted. When she went to tell her mother, her mother didn't believe her and kicked her out of the house. Tiffany had fights with women all through middle school and high school. This explained a lot to me about her sexual behavior and how she talked to ladies. I had faith in her. I believed that if I showed love, that change would happen for her. I continued to extend myself to her. For our vacation, we went shopping together for all new everything: swimsuits, outfits for every day, and shoes. I even got my hair braided by her hairdresser in the same town where she lived.

When I returned home from our shopping, I got inspired as we got ready for our Jamaica trip to find out where Christians hung out on their vacations. Where did they go for fun? What cruises were they on? I began to look this information up and found out there was a lot going on with my Christian brothers and sisters. I was pleasantly surprised that there were Christian boat rides, Christian bikers, and skate night for believers that had Christian music. There was a lot of information out there so that I desired to create a Christian website called Believer To Believer. I also continued to write poetry. I had enough poems to self-publish my first book. I reached out to one of the workers from my real estate company who was good at design to create invitations for my first book signing. While she worked on the invitation, I looked in the phone book to contact different Christian schools that had Christian dancers who would be able to come and minister for my guests at no charge to me.

Everything was set in motion. I orchestrated for my very first book signing event to be held in an Italian restaurant where I frequently visited. They had a separate area within their restaurant located downstairs where they host events. This was major for me. My poetry event included a live DJ, seven praise dancers, all you can eat buffet of pasta, salad, salmon, and chicken. The room was filled with about twenty-five people including a few of my neighbors, Brandon, coworkers from both jobs, and my first cousins who reside in New York. Brandon even paid for my mother's flight so that she could be in attendance. The night of my event I had a beautiful light blue dress. A dress that I had worn to a wedding. When I went to pick up my dress from being dry cleaned it was two-toned colors. I had to change dresses at the very last minute. I had no time to get upset so I simply changed my dress to this long black dress that seemed more appropriate for this type of occasion. I wore my hair back in a long ponytail. My mother and I got picked up in a black limousine from my apartment to take us to my event. One of the perks of working at the hotel. We used this limousine company for many of our guests and as a show of appreciation, the driver offered to drop both my mother and I off for free. We were traveling in luxury and style.

Brandon was supportive of me and whatever I desired. He sat at the table next to me and my mother. He sat and ate, and enjoyed laughing at my mother when she was up reading from one of my poems from my book. But Brandon decided to leave early because one of the songs that the DJ played from my list reminded him of the morning I served him the divorce papers. That day, I had gone to Brandon's house to take him to a restaurant so that we could have breakfast. I sat on his lap to help him tie his boots. He rode with me to the restaurant. We ordered our breakfast and when I told him that I had the divorce papers, he asked to see them. When I came back to the restaurant to hand him the papers, he signed them and then he said that he had lost his appetite and was ready to leave. When we got back in the car, I had the same song that was playing at the event.

Before he got up from the table, he handed me his credit card to pay for the balance that I owed to the restaurant for the no shows. I didn't have the money, as I was counting on those people to come. Brandon heard me venting about the no shows and immediately offered to pay the balance what-ever the balance to go on his credit card. He got up from our table and handed me his credit card. I excused myself to walk him to his truck to say goodbye. I went back to the restaurant to continue with this event. My friend from my real estate job was next to read two poems from my book and then it was my turn. I cried for most of my poem reading, which included five poems. I cried all the way through. When this event was over, I handed the restaurant owner the cash I had and Brandon's credit card. My mother said that Brandon had a heart for me. It was easy for someone to give to you when they had a heart for you. Once the event was over, my mother and I rode with our family to their apartment in New York City.

CHAPTER TWO

Agony

I walked up to the brick building prepared to take my real estate exam. I studied hard and devoted my time to make sure that I passed this test. I walked into the exam room, sat at the desk having great expectations. I was looking forward to this moment. To obtain my real estate license would change my life drastically. When I finished the test I handed my paper to the lady who was sitting at the reception desk. I waited patiently to hear the results. I felt confident in my answers. When the administrator came back to me I took a deep breath. I looked on the screen to see that I had failed the test only by a few points. It was devastating to know that I hadn't passed again. This had to be one of the biggest disappointments of my life. I shook my head in disbelief and embarrassment. I went back home adamant to study harder than before. I would try again. I went back to that same building two weeks later to take my real estate exam just to walk back out the building as a failure yet again. How could this be? It didn't make any sense that I was always short a few points of passing. I didn't want to look like a failure in my bosses eyes so I never told her about my test results. I kept it all to myself and whenever she asked I dodged the question. I came to realize that this was just not happening for me. I made a decision to never take my real estate test ever again. It was time to let that idea go.

I could really use a break and a break is what I received from King Jesus. My vacation trip was here. I had no worries about what was to come. I was looking forward to sand in between my toes, the sun, and being free. My only expectation was to have a relaxing and fun time with my best friend Olivia and with Tiffany. I met Tiffany at her place of employment to leave my car in there parking lot. Tiffany's sugar daddy came to pick us up to drive us to the airport. Tiffany and I couldn't contain our excitement. We met my best friend and two of her lady friends at a connecting flight and we all flew together to Jamaica. When we touched down in Jamaica, it was surreal from the scenery as we rode through dirt roads. The fresh air was refreshing and our resort was breathtaking. When we got dropped off at our resort we quickly ran to our rooms. I shared a room with Tiffany and one of the ladies my best friend brought. Olivia wanted me to share a room with her especially since we hadn't seen each other in quite a while but I decided to stay in a room with Tiffany since I was the only person she knew on this trip. I didn't want Tiffany to feel abandon.

We all changed our outfits so that we could walk around the resort and go to a restaurant. The first night on the resort was heavenly. I couldn't help but notice that the resort was empty. The other ladies noticed it too as they ushered one of the resort greeters to ask where were all the people? The greeter said that we just missed everyone. All of the half-naked men had just left and we came just when everyone had left. I smiled within while the other ladies looked like someone spoiled their trip. We decided to go for a swim in the pool. I was doing flips and handstands while the other ladies played volleyball. We then walked around the resort taking it all in and taking plenty of pictures together. It was a dreamlike moment for us. I thanked God that He allowed me to inhale such beauty.

The next day we got up early to eat breakfast. As Tiffany and I were getting ready somehow she and I got into a huge argument. We were loud enough that Olivia heard us in her room. She came over to find out what was the trouble and to break us up. Tiffany and I exchanged some heated words which were our first fight. Olivia intervened to separate us. We went to breakfast but separately. Olivia was with me while the other two ladies stayed close to Tiffany. In the mid-afternoon, we went back to the room to change clothes to get ready for a show that the resort was putting on. I tried to talk to Tiffany rationally when I seen her on the steps, but she wasn't interested in talking to me. I walked away kind of surprised that she didn't want to mend our relationship while on this trip. For the rest of the trip, Tiffany and I didn't speak nor hang out together. Olivia spent time with me sometimes. But I met a handsome man as I laid on a hammock reading my Joyce Meyer book. I brought this book for days when I made time for downtime. This tall handsome man told me that he watched me the first day when all the ladies were in the pool. I hadn't noticed him which surprised me because this gentleman was fine as wine. He was tall, light brown skinned, with perfectly straight white teeth. He was also from Philadelphia which wasn't far from New Jersey. We hung out every single day throughout the trip. He was like an angel sent from heaven to keep me distracted. God sent this man to me so that I wouldn't feel left alone while the other ladies enjoyed this trip together.

When we returned back to New Jersey I called Brandon to pick me up from the airport since I refused to ride with Tiffany. Tiffany and I walked away from each other without speaking as if we never knew each other. It was a hot mess but I thank God that her attitude did not ruin the blessed vacation that I enjoyed to the fullest.

I went to church that Sunday of my return back home. At the end of church service, my pastor announced that the church was starting a Bible Institute where we could earn our associates and master's degree. Some of the classes would be held in our church sanctuary while other classes would be held in our high school building which is right across the driveway. All of a sudden I could see myself taking these classes and finally passing. My heart's desire was to be in ministry full time. I knew in my heart that these classes was the start of something special in my life. These classes would help to train me to be in ministry. I was revived.

I decided to make my hotel job part-time so that I could enroll in three classes. Ultimately I had to drop one of my classes because I was way over my head. I continued with two classes sitting in the front row and asking questions. I was into this. When I had taken my final exams I passed. This was my element. I found my groove in a place where I could soar high. God closed one door to obtaining my real estate license to open another door that was a better fit for me.

I continued to enroll in classes. Making this my top priority. In one of my classes, there was this young lady who asked me a question about Christians drinking alcohol. I felt like this question came out of left field. Somehow we all ended up talking about Christians and alcohol.

From my views, I didn't see anything wrong with Christians drinking alcohol to include that I had scriptures to back up my belief. I told her that Jesus made wine out of water at a wedding. Through my eyes, there were plenty of Bible referencing Believers being able to drink wine. Why did the Bible reference that? She went on to ask me, what if I was drinking in front of someone who was a recovering alcoholic. If that person saw me drinking, they would think that it was okay for them to drink, and would relapse. Would I want to be that person who was responsible for someone's falling? Well, I never thought about that. From that point on I wondered if I should or shouldn't drink alcohol. I would have a hard time being the cause of placing a stumbling block in front of a person. I concluded after struggling within myself that I would not partake in drinking any kind of alcohol until I was certain about where I stood in this matter.

It was our last night in one of my classes when my teacher said that he was leaving to go to Africa to evangelize. During the class, the teacher said that he had a dream that one of us sitting in his class was going to have many books published.

He was laughing while reading the books. I had this feeling that dream was about me. I had written a book and was in the process of writing another book. After class, one of the students asked the teacher if we could pray for him for his safe travels to Africa which the teacher agreed. The students that stood closer to him laid their hands on him while the rest of us extended our hands towards his direction. As one of the students prayed over the teacher I had my own prayer that I was saying softly to myself and God. I prayed that if there was anyone in this class that was not fully walking with God and had evil ways that their prayers would not touch our teacher and that person would start to cough and choke. I said this prayer about three times when a man began to cough and choke. He kept on coughing and choking throughout the prayer. I opened my eyes to look up because I wanted to know who was that coughing and choking. It was one of the men who worked in the church. He attended church every Sunday and seemed to be a nice man with good intentions. I was blown away. When the other students stopped praying I went to the teacher to tell him what I had done. All the teacher said was thank you with a smile. I never revealed who this student was. I just kept my eyes on that student wondering his secret sins.

I walked away astonished that I said such a prayer and that God granted that prayer. The more that I prayed and spent time with God about others, and desiring for Him to reveal more to me, He was revealing more about myself. I was changing at a nice pace that was pleasing. God was changing me from the inside out. He had a great way of doing it. It was with a lot of love, patience, and grace with mercy. A nice speed that didn't overwhelm me.

I went to church on a Sunday with a brand new silk type of blouse that was given to me as a gift. The top portion of the blouse had a slight opening that revealed a small portion of my upper boob. I thought since it didn't reveal much that it was okay for me to wear to church but as soon as I stepped foot inside the church I was uncomfortable. As if people were watching and judging me but when I looked around no one was paying me any attention. Right before heading into the sanctuary to be seated I stopped a lady to ask her if she had a safety pin so I could pin my shirt together. When I pinned my shirt together I felt at ease.

I was at home one evening pondering if I was paying my tithes and offerings the way that God had outlined in the Bible. I was taught as a little girl the importance of giving God my first. I found myself giving excuses as to why I couldn't commit to God's commandments. I had bills and surely Jesus could understand that. But now that I had given my life to God I found myself wanting to be obedient to God's commandments little by little. I reached out to Linda who worked at my real estate office how I should give my tithes and offerings because I couldn't quite understand it fully. I felt a sense of comfortability with Linda. Often times she would bring her Bible to work to study on her lunch break. Once she gave me suggestions on what Gospel and Christian radio stations to listen to.

I admired how she dressed so I complimented her on her outfits. Once she came to work with two bags full of clothes to give to me. She told me that she cleaned out her closet and thought to bring me the bags of clothes. I was delighted and appreciative. With gentleness, she pointed out the scriptures that mentioned the significance of giving God ten percent of our first fruits. When we finished talking I knew in my heart that I had to be faithful. It didn't take me long to be consistent in paying my tithes and offerings the way that God had intended for His child to do which is according to scripture. I wanted to make God happy with my obedience and dedication.

At home, I would get emotional reading the different stories in the Bible. I would think that God could do some of the same miracles and allow us to experience a lot of the same blessings here on earth. I was fascinated by the story of the burning bush and God speaking through a donkey. Surely God would allow me to experience something similar to these.

During my walk with God, my behavior when dealing with people could use some changes as well. I never really saw that I had an attitude problem before my walk with Jesus. But the more that I walked with God I felt convicted when I finished talking with someone. One would say that I should have noticed that I had a problem when I would get fired from my past jobs for back talking my bosses or when I would get into heated arguments with my siblings, and threaten to fight on occasion or the fact that I was separated from my husband and part of it was because of my bad attitude. Walking with God I could see my problems more clearly. Often I found myself apologizing to people because of the way I spoke to them. Once I got upset with one of our deacons of my church. When I asked him if I could use one of the empty rooms in the church to practice my poetry and singing he refused me. Sure I was new to the church at that time but I was paying my tithes and offerings. I got so offended that I mailed a letter to the pastor complaining about this deacon. As I dropped the yellow envelope down the chute of the mailbox, I regretted it and wished I could have pulled the letter back, but it was too late. The damage was already done. I went to church and I sensed that word had got around so people treated me a little different. To make matters worse, I noticed that I wasn't receiving the promotions for our Bible classes. It seemed that someone took me off the mailing list. I wanted to stop going to my church, and after a few attempts, God led me back. This was my church home and it was my responsibility to allow God to change and reveal things about me, and in time it would get better. I apologized too many times to my deacon by email. He kept his distance from me which I didn't blame him. Perhaps in time, he would forgive me.

Driving back home from a long day's work I looked in my rearview mirror to see a truck driver driving too close to my bumper. I got out of my car when the light turned red, walked towards this truck driver and began to wave my neck and finger at him, screaming at him to not drive so close to my car. I was serious and all he did was look down at me smiling like I was a joke. I walked back to my car like I wish he would try me. Shortly after this incident, I was driving on that same road heading the opposite way, when all of a sudden a man in a small car tailed me, honked at me and turned into every lane I turned in.

When I looked in my rearview mirror, he looked angry at me and looked crazy. I didn't understand why he chose my car to drive behind like a maniac, but I called the police after I noticed that this man was not giving up. When I was talking on my cell phone, the police officer instructed me to turn into the nearest strip mall. If this man followed me into that parking lot, then we would know for sure that he was following me. When I turned into this public parking lot, while the police officer was still on the telephone, the man stopped following me. When I looked at his car passing by me, he seemed to be yelling at me. It was weird and not warranted. At that moment I realized that I better tone down my attitude before I attract more psychos. As a woman of God, I learned to treat people the way that I want to be treated. I had a lot to learn but this was the beginning of self-improvements.

My Faith

Brandon called me to let me know that he was being deployed. He served in the Air force Reserved and they needed him. He couldn't tell me where he was being deployed. All I knew was that he would be away for six to nine months. My mindset changed in an instant. I wanted to be as supportive as possible. The divorce would have to be placed on hold until Brandon returned back to New Jersey safely.

While he was preparing to leave, he put me in charge of paying his bills and look after his car and apartment. I asked Brandon if I could decorate his apartment while he was gone. His apartment felt dark and cold with the black leather couch and black rugs. I wanted to brighten up his place and put some small touches that would transform his apartment into a warmer place. He gave me permission as long as I stayed within a budget. I dropped Brandon off at the airport where there was another air force officer. In the parking lot, Brandon leaned in for a goodbye kiss.

While Brandon was away serving our country military support for families organization reached out to me by telephone to check up on me. They wanted to make sure that I was safely okay and ask me if I needed anything while Brandon was away. I was taken aback, as I was not prepared for a support system to call me. This was a pleasant surprise that I deeply appreciated. They reached out to me several times during the time Brandon was away. I felt encouraged and loved. This support system gave me the assurance that everything was okay. They lifted up my spirits and I appreciated our military for having such a support system it works. I wished that everybody around me was just as supportive.

Unfortunately, this was not the case. My boss, whom I used to adore in my real estate job, was not concerned for me. Her ugly side was displayed and I wished I had fair warning. Whenever Brandon would call me, I would politely excuse myself from my desk to have our conversation in private. I was never away from my desk for more than ten minutes. He could only call me during specific times and only for a certain amount of time. When I would return to my desk, my boss would give me this ugly stare. She even went as far as to tell me that her husband once was deployed and his absence was not as hard as I made it out to be. She knew that I never experienced anything like this. I was so proud of Brandon and I wanted to be supportive. I never discussed with him my frustrations about my boss or how difficult she had become. I didn't want to cause any more stress to him than what he was experiencing.

He shared with me that the place where he was, was hotter than hell. He felt like his sergeant was giving him a hard time because he was moving slower than the others. They were expecting a lot out of Brandon since he was their leader. I had to continue to show him love and speak encouraging words to him to strengthen him, keep his mind at peace, and for him to stay strong, try to work hard, and have faith. This was what I said to him weekly, and for me to get the mean stares and evil words from my boss was the most unsympathetic thing anyone had ever done to me in my time of needing sympathy.

After his six months of deployment, I picked up Brandon from the airport and dropped him off at his apartment. He was away for only six months but it felt longer. During his time away, he mentioned to me over the telephone that he didn't want me to make any sudden moves when he returned home regarding our divorce. He told me to get my mind right, but my mind was already right and set. I had a hard heart and nothing changed that. I just put things on hold but had every intention of continuing our divorce when he returned.

Brandon appreciated me for taking care of his apartment while he was gone. He invited me to his place to show me how he appreciated me. He ordered pizza and we had a pizza party on his living room floor. He wanted me to spend the night and so I did to appease him. We made love that night, but I returned home the following morning before he opened his eyes. God gave me a dream. Brandon believed that we would reconcile. God showed me that I was going to break his heart. I knew by this dream that I had to withdraw from Brandon. My motives were never to reconcile although I had given him that impression.

A few months later I stood in front of the judge in court, he asked me if I was sure that this was what I wanted. He continued to ask me if we tried everything in our power to save our marriage. Both questions I answered with a yes, but then he asked me if Brandon knew that I was in court. I wasn't sure. We didn't discuss it, however, I did serve him the papers that he signed, and he helped pay for the divorce process. He knew this day would come, so the answer for me was yes. As I looked in the eyes of the judge, he looked back and slammed his gavel down, and just like that, we were divorced. It was much easier for us to get divorced than it was for us to get married. The process for us getting married was difficult, as I had many signs not to move forward with our marriage, which I totally ignored. I assumed that I would hurt Brandon's heart by saying no when he asked to marry me. When in reality I hurt him more by divorcing him.

I called Brandon to let him know that our divorce was final. I told him that he was officially a single man. He didn't take that revelation lightly. He stayed quiet but then asked if he could come over. Maybe he figured that we both needed each other at that moment. We made small talk when he arrived and hooked up. This time our hookup felt unnatural like I was on my menstrual or something. It just felt nasty and uncomfortable. This had never happened to us before. We didn't talk about it, but we both knew that we had to stop. Brandon stayed over only for a few minutes before he left. When he left, I decided to go to sleep. When I woke up, I noticed that I had small and big, gross, nasty-looking bubbly bumps covering my entire upper body, including some bumps on my butt and face. It scared me enough that I jumped in my car and rushed to the nearest pharmacist. I ran to that counter, but the pharmacist couldn't suggest anything for me. He didn't know what I had, so I left that pharmacy with nothing in hand to cure it. It confused and shocked me that these terrible bumps were covering the only parts of my body that didn't have scars from my childhood chicken pox. The only part of my body that was scar-free, and in the summer I could show some skin. In my confusion, I had a thought that these bumps were the result of sin. God always honored our marriage even though we were separated. Once we were divorced there was nothing for God to honor therefore I sinned. I repented and asked God for forgiveness. The very next day those bumps were gone. I only had a few scars left as a reminder. The bumps put me in the mind of leprosy that they mention in the Bible.

I decided that it was best that I move forward without having any type of relationship with Brandon. It was just keeping both of us from moving on with our lives. Brandon and I didn't see each other again and we rarely spoke over the telephone. I was committed to moving forward in the Lord, and my chapter with Brandon was over. I prayed for Brandon. I prayed that he would forgive me for breaking his heart and for moving forward with our divorce. I prayed that God would bless Brandon with a good woman who would be there for him through thick and thin and that she would treat him good.

My boss at the real estate company was difficult to work with. She was being petty over every little thing. She was not that understanding and she was criticizing my work. I really got offended when she told me not to put "have a blessed day" at the bottom of my signature email, even if I was sending it in-house. If my coworkers who I had been working with for two years didn't mind, then why did she care?

Linda gave me great advice. She told me to respect my boss's wishes. She continued to say that this is the workplace and we had to work unto man and follow their instructions. I could see her point, but I was still feisty and wanted to prove my point. I went to my boss to let her know that I respected her wishes, but I didn't agree with them, especially when my coworkers didn't have a problem with it. I found it ridiculous when, out of nowhere, she asked us to send her our graduation certificate from high school. I found this convenient timing since she was all of a sudden an English professor correcting my punctuation every time I sent an email to the clients as if my emails were terrible. I had been sending the same emails with the same punctuation for two years. If the few clients I had left didn't complain, then why was she making a big deal out of it? She was getting on my last nerves. It seemed unfair treatment because I didn't see her acting like this towards the other ladies in our department. We used to have such an awesome relationship, and for it to turn sour was a disappointment.

I stepped away from my desk, as usual, to head downstairs to chat it up with some of the ladies while they made their morning coffee. Santrese told me to look up the stairs where my boss was peeking down at me like she was making a mental note. I worked hard every day that I came to work. I didn't need her foolishness. As if it wasn't bad enough that my work responsibilities slimmed down tremendously, due to the recession, the clients weren't sending transferees out to the States from other countries. A lot of my clients moved back home, which caused my workload to be slim to nothing. I went from having so much of my work to do to helping my team file their paperwork. I stayed hopeful that my workload would pick up and that I'll be busy again. Until then my days were slow and boring.

I was so upset with my boss for making my day horrible that I called Santrese to meet me in the filing closet to discuss it. Santrese was having issues with her boss, too, at the same time. To me, both bosses were making it obvious that they were trying to do something. We caught them whispering and looking at us. We weren't in that filing closet for more than ten minutes when I sensed my boss standing outside, listening in on our conversation. I motioned for Santrese to continue to talk while I tiptoed to the door and then I swung that door opened fast. I could hear my boss running inside the other filing closet, adjacent to the one Santrese and I was talking in. I became upset that she would stand outside, invading my privacy. Santrese and my conversation were over at that point.

I walked back to my desk, and then my boss came back to her desk shortly after me. She had to walk past my desk to get to hers. As she was passing, I could see that she was fired up, and I was steaming mad too. I could hear her typing hard as if she was typing an email to her boss about me. So I decided to type an email too in my defense. I wasn't thinking clearly, just moving off of my emotions.

Her boss called me into his office. When I got there, my boss was there, sitting in a chair. When we talked I could see that the conversation was not in my favor. I tried hard to defend myself, but it was going nowhere. Without even a write-up, I was told to pack my things up, go home, and never return to work again. And just in a moment, I was fired from the job God gave to me. I didn't get the chance to say goodbye to my coworkers who became my friends. How embarrassing, yet I left that parking lot with my head held high. This was a bittersweet moment. On the one hand, I would miss this place. On the other hand, my work became boring because I had no work. I was filing paperwork. I stayed positive. I had so much faith that in no time I would find a new job. God would help me. I had no worries.

I filed for unemployment also continued working part-time at my hotel job, and I continued to take Bible classes. I was steady, hopeful, and prayerful that doors of opportunity would arise. No worrles came to mind. We had a new general manager at my hotel job after the previous general manager got fired for letting a guest stay in his room with a balance of owing the hotel over $2,000. The new general manager did not like my work schedule. I switched my schedule so many times that the new general manager was losing patience and willingness to help me, although I tried to remind him that I had been working for that location for three years. I fought hard to continue to hold on to that job. It was the longest I had been at a job, so I didn't want to lose it.

Santrese called me to let me know that the real estate company was laying off a lot of people in different departments. She felt there was some injustice going on, due to the fact that she was the only person in her department who was let go. We felt that her boss and my old boss had something to do with that. They just seemed like two evil twins. While she tried to figure that out, she wasn't concerned about her finances. She had savings, she invested, and she would later file for unemployment. She had no desires to move fast in finding a new job. She would take this opportunity to live her life. She would spend more time with her family, vacation, and enjoy life for a change. She felt that she worked for so long that this was her opportunity to live her best life. I agreed. I believed that if she was happy with taking some time off and not rushing to go back to work, then kudos to her. If she had the money to do that, then so be it. I liked that she was able to do just that.

My reality was slightly different. I had no savings, and my unemployment was not enough for me to handle my bills. My car was repossessed by my friend. I was getting eviction notices and electricity shut-off notices. I could still see the light at the end of this tunnel. It was only a matter of time when God would come to the rescue.

I went on two job interviews with no job offer, which was strange to me. I would usually ace an interview and be offered the position before I made it back to my car. I wasn't sure what was going on. I didn't care that there was a recession. I always believed that my faith would overcome a recession. My faith would take me to new levels. God would miraculously bless me with another opportunity. No way would God allow me to lose my apartment. No way would He allow that to happen to me. I paid my tithes and offerings. I was faithful in attending church. I was a faithful woman of God. God would come through as He did for my mother.

Instead of giving up, I held onto my faith while sitting in my bathroom with my electricity off in the winter. I was cold when I spoke to my mother over the cell phone. My mother said that I was born for such as a time as this. She also told me that sometimes Christians had to go through what the world had to go through because we had to be that example of who we pray to. I got my power turned back on, but that didn't stop the eviction notices coming, nor the shut-off notices. I was barely surviving. I wasn't in denial, just in faith and hope that God would do a miracle for me and come through as He did for my mother.

I no longer had a car so I thought that I could afford to rent a car from one of those rental car places. I felt like that was in my budget, but this was far from the truth. I had that car for a month before they instructed me to return the car and find my own way back home. They told me in a stern voice that I was not allowed to rent from their company ever again. I sat in their lobby crying to my mother, asking her to send me a couple of hundred dollars to make the payment, but she did not have the money. I didn't know what to do, but something told me to call Santrese. One of the salesmen felt sorry for me and drove me back home. When I called Santrese, she was upset to find out all the issues I was having. She quickly offered to pick me up and let me borrow her second car. She told me that I could keep it for as long as I needed.

When she came to pick me up, she gave me terrible advice to lie and cheat to make my ends meet. I never considered doing that before, but I did what she suggested. Only after lying and cheating for two weeks, I felt guilty and stopped it. I told myself that my mother did not raise a child to do such evil just because I felt desperate to hold onto my apartment. I had to stop before I got caught and I would be one of those people. I repented and just stayed hopeful that God would perform a miracle.

In the parking lot of my Bible Institute, before we headed into class, I confided in two of the students whom I had befriended about the hard time I was having finding a job. I told them that my resume was unparalleled to others. I couldn't understand for the life of me why I didn't get any callbacks. I had been diligently seeking employment. This was a weird time for me. That was when one of the ladies mentioned to me that her employer was hiring and that she would put in a good word for me. She told me to apply online. She felt confident that someone would call me. She worked in that law firm for twenty years, so her word was golden. She didn't recommend people to her employer, so she trusted me. She trusted that I wouldn't make her regret it. I assured her that she wouldn't regret her decision to help me out.

After class, I went home to look up her law firm online. The following week of me sending them my resume, someone called me to set up an interview. During my interview with one of the partners, he mentioned to me that his son and I worked at the same apartment complex at the same time, according to my resume. His son was our pool attendant. I remembered his son vividly and hoped that his son remembered me. I treated him with fairness. I always checked on him to make sure that he was okay, and I made small talk with him. The partner told me that he would make his decision after he spoke to his son. The very next week I was offered a position. The partner told me that his son not only remembered me but had nothing but nice things to say about me. It just goes to show you to treat everyone equally. You never know when you may need them.

When the partner said that I would be working in the evictions department, I was slightly uncomfortable. It was strange for me to work in that department when I was receiving eviction notices from my apartment management. The position was paying me less than what I was making at the hotel, but I felt like I had to grab this opportunity. I told the lady who referred me that this was the only job that offered me a position with six months of me not working. It was either this job or stay on unemployment, and unemployment. I was tired of this whole unemployment thing, so I jumped on this opportunity. I saw this as a blessing, and although I was not making enough money, somehow God would look after me and perform a miracle so that I didn't have to move or lose all of my things.

Unfortunately, the hotel job couldn't take another schedule change, so the new general manager let me go. I later found out that Sophia was pregnant. The hotel was throwing her a surprise baby shower and she wanted me to attend, but the general manager said no. I didn't leave in the best light. Even though the evictions department was truly not ideal for me, I went in being grateful and with an open mind. Maybe working at the law firm would not be a horrible thing. Maybe I was overthinking it. I had my own struggles, but this job was an opportunity for me to learn and grow. Everyone was caring to me. I was trained well and the lady who recommended me checked to see how I was doing every so often. I desired to give it all I had and not take this position so personally. But honey after I got settled, this position rocked my world from the inside out. It was by far the most challenging and heartbreaking experience. It was downright overwhelming and I wished I hadn't accepted this position. Many of the attorneys were popping pills because this was an uncommon experience. They had a massive amount of families and individuals to evict, way more than the attorneys anticipated. This recession affected the real estate market in the worst way.

We had so many people to evict from their homes that we couldn't do it alone. We had to give some files to other law firms, that was how crazy it was. I was beside myself and hiding every chance I had. I mean, I had files that were up to my neck. I could never catch up with my work. Every file represented somebody's foreclosed home that we had the duty to evict. It was our job and it was nasty. The bank hired our law firm to evict people who would not move out of homes that the bank now owned. We had a ton of families and people who lived in mansions from New Jersey to New York. Our law firm represented the East Coast and the judges were not merciful to the lawyers. They made it difficult. I watched attorneys returning to their offices, having to start all over with the process. This allowed the homeowners to reside in their homes longer. I had seen people stay in their homes six months without paying the mortgage because the laws were changing too many times. New Jersey was definitely in favor of the tenant. Shoot, I gave some homeowners even more time by placing their file all the way at the bottom. Especially those who had children and the ones who served on 9/11.

I almost couldn't handle hearing a child running to the moving truck as her family was getting locked out of their home. The child forgot an item in the moving truck and cried out for them to open the door to get her stuff. I went to the bathroom and hardly could breathe, wondering when God would take me out of this misery. I could hear God tell me to stay. I was involved in evicting people when I was about to endure my own eviction. My pay wasn't enough for me to continue to stay in my apartment. Although I kept the faith, I told Santrese what was happening. I hadn't packed a thing and the sheriff was coming to kick me out in less than a week. Santrese urged me to allow her to help me. She had a friend with a truck who could help move me out at a reasonable cost. She said that I could come and stay with her for as long as I needed, rent-free, and I didn't have to help her pay bills. She said that she had a second bedroom where I could stay. At the moment it didn't have a bed, but she was in the process of furnishing it.

The day I had to go to court to try to convince the judge to allow me to stay in my apartment, and that I promised to pay the back rent, I told God that not one attorney from my office where I worked better not come up in that courtroom or I would walk out. I sat down in the courtroom along with a room full of other people who were waiting to find out their destiny. I sat down with a Christian book, reading it when I looked up to see one of the apartment managers that I interviewed with who didn't offer me a position. We made eye contact and I wondered if she remembered me. I probably wouldn't be sitting there if she had hired me. It was awkward, so I put my head down and continued reading. When it was my turn to face the judge, he told me if I did not have the money that day to pay the rent, he could not force the landlord to let me stay in my place. He had no other option than to honor the landlord and evict me. He even apologized and just like that, I was evicted.

Here I was staying hopeful, praying, and now my day had come to be evicted. I quit my job at the law firm without an explanation. I only called them to get my final check. I drove home to see a rainbow. The rainbows reminded me of the promises that God gave to me. However, I didn't feel that God kept His promise to me, and I didn't want to see that rainbow. It was the second one He gave me. He gave me one when I was fired from my real estate job which I appreciated and smiled. But this rainbow, I felt He didn't keep His word and I told Him that I didn't care about that rainbow and turned my head away in tears and anguish. Santrese guy friend with the truck came to help me pack up my belongings. I gave him my new washer and dryer and computer. I ordered us some pizza and we were moving out the morning of my eviction.

CHAPTER THREE

Crossroads

When I moved out of my apartment and packed my things, I felt like I had been defeated. I was drained and not in the right headspace to do anything but rest my soul. The day of my move, besides ordering pizza to feed this man who helped move me at the last minute, I gave him some of my furnishings along with my new washer and dryer. When I moved into Santrese's apartment, I was broken. Santrese was gracious when I moved into her home. She welcomed me with open arms ten times more than what I could have expected. She promised me that she would get a bedroom set and decorate the second bedroom for me, but in the meantime, I would have to sleep in the living room. She gave me permission to sleep on her brand new sofa, but I remembered how my mother's couch looked after her children slept on the couch. I opted to sleep on her living room floor.

She constantly had houseguests. All of her family members lived close, so apparently, Santrese home was the place to be. They came to meet me, which I thought was sweet, but they stayed to laugh and talk to the late hours of the night. When 9 pm came, I was ready for her company to go. God only knew, or maybe I gave it away in my face if someone really looked, I was coming to my breaking point. Before I could get to that point of giving up, Santrese had a bed in that second bedroom, decorating it day by day. This filled my soul and spirit. I thanked Santrese and God for showing me favor and blessings.

Santrese and I had a heart-to-heart discussion when I first moved into her place. I told her that I was not going to look for work. All I wanted to do was focus on finishing re-publishing my first book. When I finished with the process, then I would look for work, but I couldn't promise a day of completion. Santrese said that I could stay in her home rent-free, not paying any bills. She promised to take care of me and all of my needs. I was grateful and not stressed. I found a new publishing company that was willing to publish my book at no cost. When I was going through my eviction process, I was inspired to continue to write poetry. When I got to work on one of my many breaks, I stumbled across a publishing company after Googling. I submitted my manuscript and it got accepted. They needed fifty poems from me to move forward. Thank God that He inspired me to keep writing because I had that exact amount. I used Santrese's laptop, located in her room, to communicate with my publishing company for my book, and the publishing company for the new website, Believer To Believer.

I drove Santrese's car one final time to pick up my last paycheck before she gave her car to her nephew. As I was driving back to her apartment at night. I came to a stop at the red traffic light when a car pulled up right beside me. I turned in its direction and noticed two men were in the car. The driver had the face of a monster. My eyes were fixed on his monster face that was huge. His head was big and evil. He looked past me, in my direction but towards the hill, maybe to see if any cars were coming, because the next thing I knew, he ran the red light. Whatever he was about to do or whatever he had done was pure evil, and I could see it on his face. That blew my mind. I came to Santrese townhouse to tell her all that happened and to give her money towards a bill, which was the first and last time I ever gave her money.

Santrese loved to shop. Shopping was this girl's hobby. If she was not taking care of her ill family member, she was shopping, spending tons of money. I joined her on her many shopping adventures, but as time would go by, I desired more and more to stay in my room. Every day I would watch and listen to the Christian networks, Pastor Joel Osteen, Bishop T.D. Jakes, Paula White, Pastor Creflo Dollar, and Zachery Tims. I promise you that Zachery Tims was Will Smith's twin. Even their mannerisms seemed to be the same. Pastor Zachery Tims was one handsome pastor who had a gift for preaching. I looked forward to someday meeting him. I also talked over the telephone to my Christian friend from Oklahoma. We laughed and talked about God and our future. Since I moved far away from my church. I decided that I wasn't ready to attend. I called my church to let them know. They disagreed, but this was my choice. I felt like Moses on top of the mount to be closer to God and listen to God's instructions concerning my life. Although the people didn't understand me and laughed at me. I knew in my heart what I was doing without knowing all the details.

Santrese treated me to dinner every night by taking me out to some fancy sit-down restaurant. It had become our routine to go to New York and eat at BBQ's. This restaurant became my top favorite. I had their BBQ every time while Santrese ate their Texas-size wings. They had the best food on the planet. They always had a packed house. But one night of our many trips there, I was not in the mood to eat my food. I think I ate a portion of my cornbread, but that was it. I took my food to go and had plans to eat it when we got home. On our way out of the restaurant, there was a man sitting on the pavement, asking for food. Without a thought, I gave him my food, a full meal. Santrese couldn't believe that I handed this man my entire meal. Unbeknownst to me, this action planted a seed.

Santrese and I had good times whenever we spent them together, with laughter and eating good food. She stayed gone most of the day, helping her ill family member recover and doing what she did the best: shopping. She was a busy lady. I went with her occasionally to her ill family member's house, but I couldn't stay long as they had a cat and I hated cats. When I was a little girl, I got chased by a cat. I had watched the Discovery Channel, specifically the episode where it taught that if you stared too long into an animal's eye, the animal would attack. I got bold and tested that theory on my friend's cat. This cat was minding its own business, sitting on the sofa while I sat on the couch. I stared into his eyes for five minutes, then the cat leaped up and chased me into the bathroom. The cat sat at the door, waiting for me. They had to pick up the cat and carry it outside in order for me to leave the bathroom.

Sitting on the balcony of Santrese's family member's house, I spoke to Brandon from time to time while Santrese stayed inside, nursing her family. Brandon was bothered that I was evicted. He even got upset with me that I closed our joint checking account. To him, it didn't matter that we were divorced. He offered for me to move in with him until I got back on my feet. This was thoughtful of Brandon but I declined his offer. I couldn't go backwards even being in my predicament. He also suggested that I move back to where my mother and siblings were living in Oklahoma City. Olivia suggested that I move back to Illinois. She not only suggested that I move in with her family but Olivia was a Regional Property Manager in Illinois for a major real estate company. She sent me an offer letter to work for her company, making the same amount of money that I was making at my previous real estate company. She also paid for a plane ticket for me to get the heck out of New Jersey. My mother begged me to move in with her. While I understood where my loved ones were coming from with the best intentions. They loved me and wanted the best for me. I respectfully declined all offers. This was my life to live. I was to do God's will not my will or anyone else will for my life. God had a plan and purpose for my life. Jeremiah 29:11 was my point of reference. The chapter and verse continued to guide me, "For I know the thoughts that I think toward you, saith the LORD, thoughts of peace, and not of evil, to give you an expected end."

Santrese's family was supportive when I moved into her apartment. They didn't seem to have a choice. Santrese had my back and always introduced me as the person who helped her when her boyfriend left her. I would tell Santrese that she didn't have to tell everybody. But as time would go on, after five months of living in her apartment rent-free, some of her family members and friends were getting jealous. Who said favor was fair? I just kept quiet about it. No one ever came to confront me. I could just discern it. As time would continue I could see that Santrese was losing patience. Whenever I discerned that I would remind her that she was helping me because that was what God had her to do.

As time went on and I was almost finished with my book and website, I drew further away from Santrese. The only time we hung out was when she came home to take us both out to eat. The process of the book and website required a lot of my time and focus. I could tell that Santrese was getting irritated with me when I wasn't accompanying her on her outings. She then began to question why I wasn't looking for work as if we never discussed this before I moved into her place. I could tell that she was resentful and gradually becoming meanly spirited towards me. Santrese restricted me from using her computer by placing time limits.

Santrese's niece was having a birthday coming up and Santrese wanted to throw her a celebration at her niece's home. Her niece was going through a lot of personal life-and-death struggles, so Santrese thought it would be great to have an intimate celebration for her niece's birthday. At this point, I had been living in Santrese's townhouse for six months and I grew close to her family. Although they may not have understood everything about me, they all respected me. At this point in time, things got heated between Santrese and me. Her funds were getting low because she kept shopping, sometimes two times a day. She not only went shopping for herself but, she spent a hefty amount of money shopping for her family. Once I offered for us to go to the grocery store to save money and cook dinner at home. That cooking at her home never happened.

With her funds running low to pay her bills on time, she was beginning to take her frustrations out on me. She was in a rage and suddenly began to yell at me, telling me to call Brandon to pick me up to get me out of her house. I was distraught by how she was speaking to me that I went to my room and shut the door. I knew one thing for sure. I was not going to be pressured to do anything that I didn't want to do. I went inside the room and prayed for Santrese. Surely God had me in her townhouse for a purpose, and because she was being obedient in taking good care of me, He would make sure that her bills got paid.

The following morning, Santrese felt bad. I could see the sadness in her eyes and hear it in her voice. She apologized to me and we went over my plan again. Not soon after this apology, Santrese had another episode of taking her frustrations out on me. I didn't know all the details of her situation other than opening a piece of mail with a shut-off notice for electricity. I told Santrese the day that she put me out would be the day that God replaced her. I kept trying to explain the reason why I was not able to look for work at the present moment. That I was all about my God's business. However, this never went well. It was like she got hot all over again.

God gave me scripture that calmed me down after trying to explain myself to everybody: 1 Corinthians 2:14, "But the natural man receiveth not the things of the Spirit of God: neither can he know them, because they are spiritually discerned." After reading this scripture, I no longer felt the need to explain myself to anybody. I just walked in confidence in God that He would make a way of escape. God gave me a brilliant idea that would cool Santrese down from yelling at me like I was a child. I had been thinking about how can I continue to pay on my storage unit that held all of my precious valuables like my couch, dishes, paintings, bed set, my entire apartment furnishings was in storage. Santrese's sister was moving into her own apartment after being released from a rehab center. She was on the road to recovery and restoration. Santrese thought it was a good idea for me to sell my belongings, but I thought to give my stuff away to her sister.

At this point, I had mourned the loss of what seemed to be my entire life and I was ready to let my things go. I had come to a place of peace and resilience like God would replace it all in due time. Santrese rented a U-Haul and we went to pick up my things along with one of her guy friends. I gave some of my things to her guy friend and the rest went to her sister which we delivered to her. The only things I kept were some sentimental pieces, the rest of my clothes, shoes, and purses. Her sister was stunned as she was not expecting good quality of gifts handed to her for free. She was overly joyful and wanted to pay me back. I assured her the pay-back was her sister allowing me to live in her townhouse. We hugged as she thanked me. Santrese and I headed back to her townhouse to enjoy a nice dinner and much-needed rest. I felt good that God allowed me to be a giver to someone who needed it. It also caused the tension to dissolve. Santrese even allowed me to reenter her room to use her computer to finish my two projects.

I gladly accompanied Santrese to get the decorations, the birthday cake, and food for her niece's birthday party. We finally sat down at a restaurant to have lunch before we continued to go to Walmart, which was right across the street from the restaurant. I ordered the chicken parmesan. When my plate came out, immediately it looked bubbly. I could sense that something was wrong with the food. I could discern in my spirit not to take one bite of it. Santrese looked at me across the table and asked me why I wasn't going to eat my food. When I told her that I could discern that something was wrong with it, she looked at me like I had two heads and proceeded to tell me that nothing was wrong with my meal. It was hot, we could see the steam still coming from the food. She tried to convince me that I was being ridiculous. I told her that I was going to return the food and I would eat a frozen meal from Walmart. Santrese looked at me funny and said that she would take my plate of food home for herself. She took her fork and swirled it in my pasta and took two bites of my food. She didn't even eat her food, she was too busy with mine.

When we left that restaurant, we barely made it to the parking lot of Walmart when Santrese ran from her car to the ladies' restroom. She was in there for a long time. She came out of the restroom holding her stomach. She told me that I was right, something was wrong with that food. She showed me bumps that appeared all over her arms. We didn't go shopping. Instead, Santrese and I headed back to that restaurant to give the food back and to ask for the return of her money. When Santrese tried to explain what I was telling her to the restaurant manager, he was looking at Santrese like she was crazy. Anyway, he gave her back her money and we went on our merry way. It felt good not to be wrong, although I felt bad for Santrese.

My website was completed. I felt accomplished to have an online ministry that Jesus helped me build and structure. All of the creative juices came from King Jesus, and of course the website team. Now I was waiting for my book to be completed and it was at its final stages. The editing was complete. My representative instructed me to find another title for my book. I prayed about the name and went to the Bible. The words, "Mercies of God" appeared to me a couple of times in the Bible. I knew that this was the new title of my book. When I submitted it to my editing team, they approved it. Now we were almost at the end.

I was thrilled and ready to share my book and ministry website to the world. I researched magazines, and newspapers, and radio stations where I could be a guest. One of the keys to being a successful author is going out to introduce your book by giving interviews. My life was headed in the right direction and I felt great about it. Santrese was cool with me for only a few months, but I could sense things were about to get heated again. She was being rude towards me.

She was allowing me to use her computer, but she restricted the times of usage. She was always trying to force me to go with her to her family's house. I could sense her talking to her girlfriend about me in a negative way when I looked out her window to see them talking. I couldn't deny that I had been living in her townhouse for nine months, not paying one bill. I understood her frustration and understood that I had been living there for a while rent-free.

I had a conversation with God and told Him that I understood where Santrese was coming from. But it was God who placed me there, it was God who was using her and surely He would take care of her for taking care of one of God's chosen people. I felt like I owed her the effort to at least look for work. When I told her that I was going to look for a job, she was pleased. She didn't hesitate to help prepare me, making sure that I looked lovely and getting me everything I asked for, to make sure that I got hired.

I went for an interview in a thousand unit apartment complex in Newark. It was two apartment complexes wrapped up in one. I went to the interview calm. I was charming and witty, just like how I use to be. I wasn't rusty. I was on point and the assistant manager made it known to me that she wanted to offer me the position. However, I declined the offer. I didn't share this information with Santrese, as I knew that she would get angry. Whenever she would inquire I would not answer. Santrese was no fool and she could see that I was not eager to look for work, so this made her angry and bitter towards me. The sweet and understanding of Santrese had become rude and cold-hearted. She lost all patience and hope towards me. Now she was talking to me all kinds of crazy. She had an out-of-town relative come to visit her. When they came to my room for the tour, Santrese introduced her to me but excused the smell, saying that it stank in my room. She said it loud enough for me to hear it, and then she shut the door and walked away. I called the shelter in Morris County to see if they had any openings. Which they did. The counselor did a phone interview and was going to schedule me for intake, but I hung up the telephone. I thought about it some more and knew that this was not my destiny. I didn't have to move into a shelter. God would find me another place.

On Halloween, Santrese reached her breaking point and told me that I had to move out. It was the middle of the night. I felt like I couldn't just be kicked out on the street with nowhere to go. It was dangerous outside. We heard that there was a gang initiation going on, where the men were randomly picking out women to punch them for no reason. Surely God would not allow her to kick me out into the streets. My cell phone rang, and it was Tiffany on the other end. She started off the conversation by telling me that God told her to call me. She called to talk to me and apologize for what happened on our trip. She told me that she was a changed woman. How she had a relationship with God. She was reading her Bible and attending church.

I told her all that had transpired with me over the course of one year with the job loss, evictions and moving in with Santrese, but now the sweet Santrese was threatening to kick me out. I told Tiffany my plans to look for work next year, as I was preparing to launch my book, Mercies of God. Tiffany heard all that I had to say and she asked me to come and live with her and her daughter. She told me that her son moved out because he was too grown to live in her house and abide by her rules. He was headed off to college and living in New York with his daddy. She told me that I could stay in his room until the beginning of the New Year. She had a boyfriend, but she assured me that he was only a visitor. I thanked her for listening to God and calling me. I accepted her offer and proceeded to rush off the phone to share the good news with Santrese. I felt energized and I had a sense of relief like God was fighting my battles and rescuing me. I could tell by the look on Santrese's face and her body language that she was disappointed. Maybe she thought that she could convince me to look for work. Her tactics to yell and degrade me didn't work. I wasn't living my life for Santrese, therefore, she couldn't dictate where I would go. I lived by God's will. Santrese drove me to Tiffany's apartment and dropped me off. I had no plans for continuing a relationship with her.

God's Will

Tiffany greeted me at the door and we hugged like friends and that we both were sorry and we forgave one another. She showed me around her apartment that was just as nice as Santrese's townhouse. Tiffany's home just felt cozy and comfortable, very homey. She introduced me to her daughter and showed me her son's room, where I would be staying. His room was just right for me. It was a perfect size, clean, and it had a comfy lounge chair that had colorful pillows. I could see myself sitting there, writing in my journal, listening to my gospel music from my portable radio.

Tiffany took me to her bedroom to show me her closet that had more shoes than I could count. This girl was a shoe fanatic. Tiffany gave me two pairs of shoes with two purses that I thought were beautiful. She joked that I had no sense of style. What I liked about the shoes that she had given to me was that they were flats. All of my shoes were heels with one pair of tennis shoes. I only brought a handful of things with me, as I had left some items at Santrese's place. Right before I was leaving, Santrese told me that I could leave my things in her closet for as long as I wanted.

Tiffany wasn't like Santrese in that Tiffany cooked meals every single night before she went off to work. She was a good cook. Her food was finger licking good. I went back for seconds and thirds until I noticed that she was making weird faces when I returned in her kitchen. I discerned real quick that I should only go in her kitchen one time for dinner. Some nights I went with her to work, as she still worked overnights at a hotel. I spent most nights in their business center using their computer sending out massive emails about my book and website.

One night Tiffany came to the business center to get me because one of her guests heard about my story and wanted to pray for me. But I quickly shut that down. I told her that I would not go to meet this gentleman who I did not know and that I did not allow just anybody to lay hands on me to pray for over me. She must've got offended because right after that her demeanor changed towards me. She was distant and hard to talk to. I kept to myself by staying in the room, listening to gospel music and writing in my journal. I also took notice that her boyfriend was not just a visitor but a resident. He was there when I woke up and when I fell back to sleep. He was a cool dude, never disrespected me. All he did was eat and play video games. I don't think that he had a job. She loved him, but for some reason, they had screaming matches once a week. She kicked him out and it seemed like too much drama for me.

One argument between them escalated where he ran into my bedroom where I was sitting on the lounge chair to tell me that Tiffany and her daughter were plotting to kick me out of their apartment before the Holidays. He shut the bedroom door to continue to tell me everything on his mind. I could hear Tiffany yelling in the background for me to not listen nor believe him. She said that he was lying but in my heart, I knew that he had no reason to lie to me. I felt that he was sincere in every word he spoke. He walked out of my room and I could hear them screaming at each other again and the front door opening and slamming shut. Tiffany came to my room to tell me that it was all untrue and that she never planned to kick me out and that she would honor her word as promised. But in the back of my head, I knew that what he said was true. I had no worries. I was in a good place knowing that God used her boyfriend to not allow Satan to use Tiffany to follow through with her plan. She went to her room to cry and I followed her to console her. This was draining, and when I went back to my room to rest, I knew that God saved me and the devil could not do what he had intended. I thanked God for showing me her true colors. I decided I would keep quiet while I stayed there, being positive.

Tiffany's attitude towards me was respectful. It was like after that fiery night both of their attitudes got checked, and not by me. It was God's doing. God had my back and I slept well at night. I could not say the same for Tiffany and her daughter. Tiffany's daughter seemed sweet in front of me, but the girl was getting kicked out of school every other week. I rode with Tiffany a couple of times when she went to her daughter's school to pick her up from being expelled. It was ludicrous. In between Tiffany's rollercoaster relationship with her boyfriend and her daughter getting kicked out of school multiple times, I knew that God had me in her home for a reason. God was doing a triple blessing. God was blessing me through her by providing for me a roof over my head and meals to eat. And I was a blessing to her by bringing peace, and the love of God.

Thanksgiving arrived and Tiffany was having a big Thanksgiving dinner at her apartment for her friends, including her boyfriend. This was the only time she didn't roll her eyes when I went in the kitchen for seconds and thirds. She even encouraged me to get more. One of her Christian friends was rather ungracious to me. She heard about me not allowing Tiffany's guest to pray over me and it rubbed her the wrong way. She asked me how I could refuse prayer. She went on to ask me silly questions, like did I highlight scriptures in my Bible and if I knew how to quote scriptures. I said no to both of her questions. I didn't have a reason to mark up my Bible. I usually wrote in a notebook or on a piece of paper. The only scripture that I knew how to quote was John 3:16. Maybe she thought that she was better than me. She sure acted that way but I kept the peace and kept a smile on my face. I was not going to entertain negativity.

From Thanksgiving to Christmas we were hanging tough. I was able to spend time handling my business in peace. I went with Tiffany to work. Her boyfriend was no longer staying within the apartment, which meant no arguing. Her daughter was managing her behavior. We went to many places together. I found it rather interesting that the same Christian friend who grilled me with questions was the same friend who went with Tiffany to a nightclub. Then Tiffany told me that her friend's husband was locking her out of the house and treating her like she was not his spouse. This made sense to me in how she was treating me. Hurt people like to hurt people.

Tiffany had a Christmas party where many of her friends gathered and we had a great time. Some of her guests I knew from back in the day when we all went clubbing, and the others I worked with. Before the party, Tiffany put lashes on me and I looked beautiful with a red shirt and black slacks. My half-wig was on point. I felt like a princess. She had a packed house. Even her boyfriend was in attendance. We just laughed and she let me eat as much as my heart desired.

I played spades with the fellas. This was one of my favorite games. I used to watch my mom and dad play this with our kinfolk down in Alabama. Playing spades is a way to bring families together in competition with a dash of fun. While I was sitting there, playing cards in the center of the living room at the table that they set up for the spades players, Tiffany and her girlfriends sat on the couch, whispering in each other's ear looking in my direction. I knew in my heart that they were talking about me. I felt it and it troubled me. I knew that it was time for me to go and move out of her apartment immediately.

I called that Shelter in Morris County after Christmas and right before the New Year's to see if they had a bed for me. We went through the telephone interview where the counselor asked me why I wanted to move into that shelter and what were my plans in life. I told her that I didn't have a choice, because after the holidays I didn't have a place to live. I shared with her all that I had gone through and that I was hopeful that my time in the shelter would be temporary, but a point of me starting my life over again. I told her that

I just published my book and that I was thrilled about that. I assured her that I would be looking for work. I had lived in Morris County most of the years that I had lived in New Jersey. Morris County had been my residence and I wanted to continue that. She understood and told me that her establishment would be happy to house a person like me.

I called Santrese to come and pick me up from Tiffany's apartment. I spent New Year's with Santrese and she tried her hardest to talk me out of moving into a shelter, even involving her sister, who I gave my furniture too. She tried to discourage me by providing information that the shelter was not how I imagined since I was acting all nonchalant about it. They had no idea that my exterior was a hard shell, but deep down inside of me I was not looking forward to it. However, I saw this as God's will type of movement. Santrese's sister told me that I had to take my belongings in bags and carry them with me all day. She said the food was terrible, the people were horrible. She pretty much told me that the shelter was not a place for a girl like me.

After speaking with Santrese and her sister, I spoke with the counselor of the single women's shelter. The counselor told me that I could only bring a bag of clothes and shoes because we were assigned lockers, which were described to me as "high school lockers." If I could imagine. We had room for a few of our belongings to be protected. I had to bring a lock because I would store my personal items in that locker. Therefore there were no toting my clothes everywhere with me as Santrese's sister said, which a relief to me was. This meant that the closet full of clothes, shoes, and purses that I had in Santee's townhouse, I could not take with me. I had too much still, even though I scaled it back. I had no time to give my clothes, shoes, and handbags away. I had to throw them away. This really hurt my soul. I loved every piece of clothing. They represented the fashionable, hard-working, person, in me. This was a painful process.

It was the dead of winter and I was glad that Tiffany gave me two pairs of flat shoes. One was a pair of black boots and the other pair of flats were a little dressier. When I was putting my items together of what I could take with me, I couldn't find one of the pairs of shoes Tiffany had given me. They looked more like Gucci shoes. Maybe she took them back. That was cold to do that to me. How do you take back a gift? I just shook my head in disbelief and continued to separate the items I could take and what to throw away. Those flat shoes sure would have come in handy.

While no one understood me, and my family and close friends fought my decision, at the end of it all, for me, this was God's will. I had no choice in the matter other than surrender to His decision. This didn't look too bright on the outside, but on the inside of me, I knew that I would be all right once I surrendered to His will.

Santrese and her niece drove me to the shelter and dropped me off. If at any moment it was the right time to cry, this would be it. I stood in the shelter's parking lot, looking at the building with one bag of my personal items in one hand, and on the other hand I had my portable radio. I could not cry. I had a sense of peace that passes all understanding. I was fine. Not one tear would come out. I was not emotional. Rather, I was brave as I was face-to-face with my destiny.

I moved into the shelter just as quiet as an introvert. When I entered the building, I had no thoughts. My bags had to get searched while I got scanned. We weren't able to bring any snacks in the building, only bottles of water. The shelter was split into two different levels. The first level housed the men of all ages. The second level housed women and children. The women's level was separated into sections. There were single women who were on a ninety-day program. Then there was the section for women who had mental issues. Further down the hall, the third section had the women with children. Their program lasted for over a year, depending on their need and availability. I was shown my room that I shared with nine other ladies from all ages and demographics. I had the choice of picking to lie on the top bunk or the bottom, which was humorous to me, since I never had a bunk bed, not even as a child. I had a bunk bed but I brought the top mattress down to the bottom to make one bed. I didn't want to share a bedroom with any of my siblings.

I went to the counselor, Masika's office to formally introduce myself. She told me that it was dinner time and to come down to the first level and have dinner with everyone. I was usually an outspoken person with a lot of energy and personality. Whenever I was in a new environment, I was always quiet, but this time I was exceptionally quiet. I went to have dinner with everyone. I did have to wait in line for my food, but it was quick. I was handed my food by volunteers. I sat at a table to myself, just looking at my food. I looked back towards my counselor, who was standing by a gentleman. She looked at me and gave me a warm smile. I turned back around to look at my food and glance at the people around me. It took me seconds to get up and throw away my food, leaving the table, not eating anything on my plate. I retired to my bunk bed and went to sleep.

The next morning I went into Masika's office to go over the shelter rules and the program policy. I handed Masika a copy of my new book. She was impressed with what I had done and thought that this was a new chapter of my life. She explained that the program was for ninety days. I had to look for work every day and turn in a form that showed who I reached out to, how I reached out to them, with the date and time. The shelter had a van that dropped us off in town where there was the workforce, to look for work and meet another counselor. In town, there was a library where a lot of the homeless folks went, and the soup kitchen with other restaurants. We had to come back to the shelter any time after 5 pm but before midnight. There were a few exceptions. We were checked every time we returned to the shelter to make sure that we were not bringing in food, drugs, or alcohol, nor weapons. They had a zero-tolerance program.

The only time we were allowed to stay in the shelter all day was over the weekend, holidays, or severe snow storms. However, the van was always available seven days a week.

The van had certain times and places where they dropped us off and picked us back up, but it was our responsibility to make sure that we arrived back by the last van. We did not have to travel with our personal things, which was why we had the locker. There were volunteers every day of the week to prepare a hot and decent meal for us. The only time that they did not show up as if we had severe weather that prevented them. During the ninety days, I had to go and sign up for food stamps and housing. Housing paid for me to live in the shelter and after the program, if I had to get an apartment or rent a room for a year. We received monthly income that was about $150, which had to last, and we got no other money except food stamps. While we were looking for work, they would set up a meeting with an organization called Dress for Success, where we would go to get dressed and sized for work suits and shoes for our interviews, and when we started our place of employment. This was a well-oil machined. I was happy that the shelter took care of the people, and treated us with respect and dignity. I was glad that God didn't have me in a place that was the opposite of this blessing. This was a sigh of relief for me mentally, physically, and spiritually.

The shelter I was in was clean and the workers were polite and showed us respect. I went back down for dinner for my second night to learn that the women and children were called to get our plates before the men. After we ate, then it was their turn. I sat down with a plate full of food, but again I was not in the mood. Another young beautiful lady with pretty brown eyes sat right in front of me, staring at me while she ate her food. Eventually, I got up to retire to bed, not eating again.

My mother miraculously received thousands of dollars on a credit card. She was able to send me $40 every so often. This money went towards food and snacks and personal hygiene. With my mother's newfound income, she was able to take care of our phone bill, which we still shared on a plan.

By the second week of living in the shelter, I met all of the single women and got along with them. I even met the young lady who sat right in front of me at dinner my second night. I call her Pretty Eyes. She was a short, petite, dark-skinned lady with a sophisticated style and straight, long hair. She was soft-spoken and ten years older than me. I could not guess her age, as she did not look a year past thirty. She had family who lived in town. Her story was quite different as to why she was living in the shelter. Unfortunately, she lost custody of her children by a wrongful penalty for disciplining her children. She moved around to different families' houses until she moved into the shelter with no place to live. She visited her family, but she couldn't live with them, which was strange to me.

She had a boyfriend who was as handsome as they came. It amused me that he allowed her to live in a shelter. Not that I condoned living with a man before marriage, but he seemed successful. Surely he could have worked out something for her. She spent a lot of time with him when she was not in the shelter or church. By just looking at her, it was hard to believe that she lived in the shelter. She had money from her unemployment to spend to her liking. She purchased an iPhone for over $400. She had expensive taste, walking around with a Louis Vuitton bag that her boyfriend purchased for her. Pretty Eyes was sweet though. She drove her mother's van to the hair supply store and she purchased a new wig and any products I needed. She was caring and sweet to me. She gave me money to make sure I had food. She even gave me a big bottle of perfume without me asking for it. This gift of perfume reminded me of the scripture Proverbs 27:9, "Oil and perfume make the heart glad, so a man's counsel is sweet to his friend."

I had a busy first month in the shelter. Everything was not always what it seemed. I made some great relationships. I went from not speaking to anyone to building friendships, walking side-by-side with them, taking advice and spending quality time with them. I helped one of the ladies take her braids out of her hair as she styled her hair differently. The food was pleasant. I was starting to gain weight eating the food that the volunteers were cooking. Along with looking for work by sending out thousands of emails to different businesses every week, I reached out to different media outlets, introducing my new book. I did a radio interview with a gospel radio station. I participated in the shelter's documentary where I was interviewed. I also interviewed with the daily newspaper in my county. We talked and the reporter was intrigued by my story. She did a two-page article about my life's journey as an author in the shelter, with my picture big on the cover. When I read the article it was about overcoming and having faith. I was proud of what I had overcome and what God did. The reporter did a great job telling my story.

Pretty Eyes was supportive of me by purchasing copies of the newspaper that she shared with her family and friends, even purchasing a few copies for me. She bragged about my success. I knew in my heart that God placed me there for a purpose. All of my hopes and dreams were about to come true. When I thought about it, I had it all and then lost it. I wrote a book to end up living in the shelter. God had my blessing coming to me and it was only a matter of time before He rescued me. I believed in my heart that it would not be too long before God showed out. With all of these opportunities to share my story, God would move on the heart of man to bless me. I would go from the shelter to the mansion. I would go from not having money to making millions. I was listening to the gospel music that kept me at peace and hopeful. I was reading my Bible to be inspired. I was faithful in continuing to pay my tithes from my $150 and attending church. I would not have to live in the shelter for the full ninety-day program. God would exceed my expectations.

CHAPTER FOUR

The Shelter

My two sisters, baby brother, and mother who live in Oklahoma City have been my rock. We've always been a close family. We moved from the state of Alabama where we were born and raised to Oklahoma City when we were teenagers to be closer to my mother's siblings. Being raised in a single parent home we were taught to share, care for each other, and have each other back. When I moved to New Jersey away from my family I kept in communication and sometimes helped my family by sending money to assist with their bills. When my mother was not able to pay her cell phone bill I put her on my plan and paid the bill for two years straight. My siblings and mother have supported me in other ways. No matter how far I've traveled we've stayed in communication. I would call them frequently to make sure that they were doing okay. I sent money to one of my sisters who is a single parent of three children. It's usually for her rent or utilities. I never wanted to see or hear about them struggling especially if I had the money to take care of it. It was easy for me to send the money without hesitation and without being asked. I felt that it was my responsibility being the oldest sibling. I also felt that they relied on the financial blessings that I was sending. I would come to the rescue and save the day without thinking twice about it. When I began to experience my own financial difficulties it was hard for me to reject them.

Whenever my mother called me to discuss their troubles I had to switch the subject. It bothered me to have to say that I didn't have the funds for them any longer but at the same time, I really didn't want to be their crutch. I was the reason why they didn't try to figure it out some other kind of way. But for them to grow and learn from their mistakes I could no longer be their god.

On this road to being a disciple of Christ Jesus, I could no longer be engrossed in certain kinds of conversations. I found myself reverting back to the old me whenever I was on the telephone with my family and with my close friends. They didn't quite understand my transformation. One of my longtime friends called me weird which hurt my feelings. As a result, I had to limit my time on the phone with them. I accepted the fact that while God was transforming me that not everyone was being transformed. In order for this trans-formation to be successful I had to withdraw and focus more on this journey, Luke14: 26 & 27, "If any man come to me and hate not his father, and mother, and wife, and children, and brethren, and sisters, yea, and his own life also, he cannot be my disciple. And whosoever doth not bear his cross, and come after me, cannot be my disciple."

I continued to stay in contact with Big Mama, Granddaddy, Grandma Iris, and many of our relatives in Alabama over the years. When we lived in Alabama we frequently visited Big Mama and Granddaddy's house. One of my favorite trips to their house was over the holidays, especially around Christmas. Big Mama and Granddaddy had presents to hand out to us little children every single time, while my aunts and uncles handed out money. I sat in their living room couch that was covered in plastic looking over the photos of us with our colorful barrettes and matching outfits. Big Mama and Granddaddy's house was the home where everyone migrated too. They had food on the stove ready for the family at all times. Most of their children lived in homes a couple of blocks away from them. They were surrounded by love.

Big Mama is what God mentions in the Bible of a vir-
tuous woman and my Granddaddy was the true role model
of what a man exemplifies in grace, ambition, how to treat
a lady, an awesome dad, and a handsome man. About the
past four years, Big Mama had old Alzheimer's disease. She
remembered me sometimes when I called. It didn't bother
me as I remembered her and that's all that mattered to me.
Granddaddy was losing his hearing. Often times I had to
speak loud where I had to go outside. They were the light of
our world even in their old age.

Grandma Iris was our grandmother who also helped raise
us. Grandma Iris cared for her grandchildren every weekend,
summers, and on Independence Day. My mother would drop
all four of her children off at my Grandma Iris apartment. I
could hear my Grandma Iris telling my mother to not leave
us all night as my mother was dropping us off and heading
out the door herself. Shoot my mother had plans to either
hang out with her man or party all night at the club with her
girlfriends.

My siblings and I didn't mind staying at my Grandmother's.
It was a tone of fun. There were plenty of kids for us to
play with around the neighborhood. Whenever my mother
dropped us off at my Grandma Iris home and if my Grandma
was praying that meant that we had to stay inside and pray
until my Grandmother finished. My Grandmother was a long
prayer. She prayed in tongues, crying, sitting on her couch
rocking back and forth. I never saw my Grandmother go to
a church but she surely had church in her apartment. She
prayed every day and her radio station was set on the gospel
and Christian radio stations. We were not allowed to turn it
to secular music. When she wasn't watching her favorite
soap opera show, she was watching a Christian network purchasing their healing rags. She always had a pan of cornbread and collard greens on the stove. There was always
plenty of food available for us to eat even extra for any of our
friends. The adults in the neighborhood of my Grandmother
would get her grocery list and money to purchase food for

her. They watched us too to make sure that we were safe. Talk about it takes a village to help raise children. The neighborhood adults were equally aunties to us as our real ones.

I had been living in the shelter for a good month when my mother called me to let me know that Big Mama had passed away. My family paid for my ticket to go to the funeral. This was not in my plans to attend a funeral while my residents were living in a shelter. This was not ideal. However, I had to be there to support my family especially my mother who took the news hard. My Big Mama lived to be ninety years old and was married to my granddaddy for over seventy years when she passed. They had a good marriage one that I would like to emulate.

I was relieved when Masika approved my travels to Alabama for her farewell. She said that I had to provide proof when I returned. My family booked me a flight and immediately I started to prepare. Pretty Eyes and I went to Dress for Success for some interview clothes prior to my hearing of my Big Mama's passing. From Dress for Success, I had a few options for the funeral. I had chosen two black suits and a light brown skirt suit. I chose the light brown suit instead of a black suit for my Big Mama's funeral. The brown represented my mood. Big Mama was a jewel. We were privileged to have such a gift from God.

I didn't know what to expect when my family arrived at the airport. I hadn't spoken to them in over a year and hadn't seen them longer than that. But when they arrived at the airport they all embraced me with hugs and kisses. My mother embraced me the most as she was emotional and happy to see her first born child. I embraced my mother and was glad to see her but I was passive. It was a lot for me to take in with my Big Mama's passing at this time of my life. However, I tried to keep my issues to myself and be present. I needed a break from the shelter although this is not the idea break nonetheless I was away.

At the funeral, my mother cried more than all of us. Big Mama made sure that my mother needed for nothing, always being her support system. Our family in Alabama helped raise us and that was because of the love that our Big Mama and Granddaddy showed us. My mother would not have been able to raise us without the help of my family in Alabama. My mother almost didn't know what to do with herself. I felt sorry for her. What were we going to do without Big Mama?

I look around, wondering where some of my cousins were, especially Kevin. When he was younger he was the funniest short boy. I didn't see his entire family. When the funeral ended, the family gathered together at Big Mama's and Granddaddy's house as usual. My Granddaddy looked peaceful sitting in his favorite chair. The aunties sat in the kitchen and dining room, talking and reminiscing, while our cousins were scattered all over the place.

The next day we met our auntie on my father's side with her husband and children at the mall. We didn't stay long, as our trip was short. We wanted to meet the new additions to our family. As we walked in the mall, one of my nieces wanted to do something that her mother told her not to. She got upset with me because I agreed with her mother. She didn't like that, so she jumped up at me, trying to act like she would hit me, with this smirk. The old me would have addressed that behavior on the spot, but the new me didn't have the energy to be confrontational.

While we were walking towards the exit of the mall, my baby sister and niece started to criticize me. I felt that the enemy used them to verbally attack me. It was all that I had not to cry. I tried to avoid them, but it was hard to disregard taunting bullies. Then our car keys got lost. My mother said in a whisper, "You cannot mess with a child of God." We had to wait for a tow truck, but I was glad when that trip was over. I went back to the shelter, grateful for the break.

When I returned to the shelter, I was greeted by Pretty Eyes and some of the ladies. One of the men said that I looked like I was living in the shelter undercover because I did not fit the idea of a person living there. Yes, I was well groomed, thanks to Jesus and to my mother, who raised her children to believe that you can take care of your appearance despite your financial woes.

There were plenty of unique stories that ended people in the shelter. There was a teacher who fell on hard times. There was a Newspaper Reporter who lived in the shelter. Pretty Eyes was another perfect example. There was a young, beautiful beautician who lived in the shelter. Man, there were so many beautiful humans with different stories living in the shelter, who you could not tell by walking past them or simply engaging in a conversation that they were homeless and struggling. Then there were some people living in the shelter with mental health issues. I would speak to a lady every morning when I was sitting on the couch reading my Bible early morning before everyone got up. This lady and I were the only ones up. I said good morning to her until she called me a bitch. All that attitude just because I said good morning. I knew at that point that not everyone was in their right mind. You had to leave them alone to prevent things from escalating. Everyone needs prayer.

There were others who were in the shelter recovering from drugs and alcohol. One of the men was a Christian who had a problem leaving the drugs alone. Often times he would come into the shelter late and get kicked out for a day or two. I had conversations with him where he confided in me his struggle. This drug use was a stronghold, yet he was a Christian man. He could not kick this bad habit. He really desired to leave it alone. Then I never saw him again. I later found out that he passed away someplace outside, alone, with drugs in his system. This broke my heart, as I wanted the best for him. I heard his true heart and I knew that if he could have left this drug world alone, he would have, but it was too late. He didn't have another chance. I prayed and hoped that I would see him again in heaven.

Then there were others who were living in the shelter as part of their rehabilitation coming from prison to the real world, where they could find work and adjust back into a new life. Now, these men were the best. I mean, they were only short of chance and opportunity. Most of them needed someone to be there for them to help change their mindset, hold their hands, walk side-by-side with them day and night and be their cheerleaders. I mean, you had to invest time and deposit something positive into their spirits in order for a resolution to take place. It was hard to do, but it could be accomplished. I noticed the ones who were a success had great family support and a new friend who was equally invested in their future by helping steer them in the right direction. Others who were left to fend for themselves and would walk this journey alone, they fell right back into their old routines because they were left alone. Those types of people I felt sorry for because they looked like lonely men, so they resorted back to their old lifestyles of drugs and other criminal activities.

One of the men who came from prison was well groomed, a nice guy and a hard worker. He managed to get a job at a donut shop. He took classes online. When I came on the scene, he always had that donut shop spic and span. It was the cleanest donut shop I ever saw, and he was friendly with the customers. Just an awesome person and he gave me a free cup of coffee with a donut. He was so happy about his future. He moved out of the shelter into renting a room. I went to visit his room, which was set up nicely. He had a bright future, but then his job was taking advantage of his situation. They were paying him minimum wages and requiring a lot out of him. The managers fired him when he began to ask them questions. He tried hard to find a new job, but unfortunately, he wasn't able to find another. As a result, he had to move out of his place. I felt bad for someone who worked hard and had good intentions. I would go back to that donut shop. The workers were not as friendly, the place was empty, dirty and dusty, the floors needed sweeping and the windows needed cleaning.

Pretty Eyes had this criminal record for spanking her child. This made it hard for her to find work with decent pay. She would be hopeful as she handed out her resume at job fairs, but once she filled out the application and admitted to a criminal past, she was rejected before they even gave her a chance. Still, she stayed hopeful and prayerful. She continued to look for work, as that was a part of our responsibility while living in the shelter. Since it was difficult for her to find a regular job, she saw this as an opportunity to pursue her dream of helping ex-offenders like herself. She decided to start a nonprofit that focused on encouraging ex-offenders while they were transitioning.

And then there was Carlos, an attractive man whose offense was selling drugs. Now Carlos had multiple kids with multiple baby mothers, that was how handsome he was and how much swagger he had. He was from New York and looked every bit of it. Carlos and I became close friends. If I wasn't hanging with Pretty Eyes, going to church, I was hanging with Carlos. We went from Work Force, sending out hundreds of emails for a job, to the library, hanging out. I knew that God placed him in my life for a purpose. He liked me, but I wouldn't entertain such foolishness. I did not come to the shelter to find love. I kept on encouraging him day and night, rooting for him, always telling him that he could do it. I never supported his bad habits. I always mentioned that he could do better than what he did in his past. I told him that God had a plan and purpose for his life. We were each other's support system.

Tim was another man who came from prison. He used to have a mansion, was married and wealthy, but drugs and alcohol caused him to lose all of that and land him in prison for doing something unlawful with his business. I invited him to church along with others, and some came with me, but Tim came to church with me every Sunday. One time I had a breakdown moment where I got tired of climbing down off of a bunk bed and I was so over standing in line for breakfast. I laid in that bunk bed, looking up at the ceiling for a couple of minutes when it dawned on me that Tim was counting on me. I hurried up and got dressed. When I finally came downstairs, there was Tim waiting for me and the church van. Tim would be in our church parking lot, smoking his cigar. I never said a word to him about that. Honestly, that didn't matter. I was glad that he was attending church with me.

There weren't too many women in the shelter from prison as part of their probation, other than Carol and Kim. Now Carol slept on the bottom bunk from me. She was smarter than your average Ivy League graduate. She knew almost everything under the sun. She was witty, smart, and just a humble soul who liked to give. She encouraged one of the ladies to bless me with that hoodie, which I appreciated. Carol always urged me to go to the soup kitchen. She said that this place was where everybody went who was homeless, and some people with low incomes.

Carol kept bugging me about going to this soup kitchen until after two months I decided to go with her and the other ladies. I never had the desire to go. As a matter of fact, I rejected the idea. It didn't sit well with my spirit. I was not looking forward to it, but to make Carol happy I went. The line was not that long, the women got to go first. The environment was clean and the food they served was lasagna and salad, which didn't taste bad. As soon as I sat down, I looked around and noticed that there were men staring at me. There was one younger man sitting next to me who later followed me to the library. Next to him was a Puerto Rican man with tattoos all over his arms and some on his face. I asked the young man who followed me to the library about the gentleman who was sitting next to him. He told me that man was in a gang and was a woman beater. From the moment I realized that the men were staring at me, then the man who followed me, and the other man I should not have inquired about, that the soup kitchen was not the place for me. I was taken care of by King Jesus when He blessed my mother, so I kept on going to the little cafe on the corner. The corner cafe was my soup kitchen. Carol didn't mention the soup kitchen to me again. She didn't take it personally. She did enjoy my gospel music, especially when I played Mary Mary's song, It's the God in Me. She sometimes sang along.

Kim was the other woman who was a part of the prison program. Kim kept to herself as she had a boyfriend and a job at the donut spot. She was a recovered drug addict and on her way to finding another place to live by saving.

Pretty Eyes boyfriend who had a luxury car dropped Pretty Eyes off at the shelter daily. I wondered what he did for a living for his girlfriend to be living in a shelter. He was sharp from head to toe. She was always with him. He even attended church with her. They were the cute couple in church. His character came into question with me when he went missing on Valentine's Day. He told Pretty Eyes that his son had a football game that he couldn't miss. I didn't believe him, but Pretty Eyes hung on to his every word. It helped her to get over her hurt when the next day he brought her a bouquet of red roses and balloons, which she displayed on her bunk bed. What kind of man lets his woman live in a shelter when he bought her a Louis Vuitton bag and gave her expensive gifts? Why couldn't he find her a place to live? What kind of man was he? I kept these questions in the back of my head. I didn't want to ruffle her feathers. Besides, she was in love with this man. She walked around like she had it going on and she stayed positive. She had a lot of faith in her future and I admired that.

Several people thought that we were blood sisters. We both were brown-skinned women who dressed superbly. I always wore my tennis shoes or black flat boots that Tiffany gave to me, with a double pair of pants, hoodie, and coat. I was well groomed but not extra. Pretty Eyes, on the other hand, wore fur hats and coats with a big red Louie bag. She and I would always get strange looks and unnecessary comments when we stood in line to get our food stamp card, but that never fazed me. I only knew about it when Pretty Eyes told me. My purpose in life was greater than people's thoughts about me.

My brother called me on three-way with my cousin, Kevin. Kevin didn't attend Big Mama's funeral because he was on house arrest, about to go to court for murder. Obviously, he wasn't the funny cute little boy anymore. He was a man. However, he was raised better than any police report and hanging out with the wrong type of people. He came from a family of love and serving the Lord. I knew that it would devastate our family in Alabama if he went to prison. I told God that I would not be able to see my family have to deal with this after the loss of our Big Mama. Most of our aunties were over fifty years old. When my cousin talked, I couldn't make sense of anything that he was saying. I could barely hear what he was saying because I couldn't fathom him partaking in murdering another human being. So I prayed a prayer that God would show him grace and favor in the eyes of the judge, that God would not allow him to go to prison and that he would be set free and given another chance at life. I told him that he could not do anything like this again nor hang with that type of people, and I reminded him of who he used to be, this funny, charismatic person. I hung up the phone after we all prayed. We had faith that God would turn his case around.

The next day he had court and the judge gave him grace. He didn't have to go to prison and he was no longer on house arrest. We worshipped God for an awesome report. God planted this message down in my heart. God told me that He gave my cousin grace. God let me know what grace meant. Grace is when you deserve what is coming to you but you don't face it. That was powerful and ministered to my soul. We hung up the telephone and I celebrated that God answered our prayer. Kevin got another chance at life again.

God Always Fights for His Children

Carol gave me some great advice while looking for a job. She told me to not accept any job with low pay because the housing assistance would immediately stop. They didn't care how much we got paid. Once we were employed, we no longer received food stamps or housing assistance. I thanked her for those words, although Masika was aggressive in trying to help us get off of assistance. I took heed to words of wisdom Carol gave me. I didn't jump on the first opportunity. I went to a few job interviews, but once I found out the pay, I was uninterested. They didn't offer me the position, but I didn't pick up the telephone to find out. I never discussed this with Masika. Whenever she asked me how my job search was going, I replied by always talking about God and what He was going to do for me. He would bless me with the perfect job at the perfect time. I talked about my faith walk, and while I looked for work I was waiting on God to bless me. At first, she understood, but after two months of not producing results of securing a job, she was not that understanding.

I was in the room talking to Pretty Eyes and the other ladies when Masika called me into her office. She asked me how my job search was going. I spoke of faith. She then instructed me to bring her the money I had saved up. She proceeded to tell me that if I did not have any money towards savings, that she would kick me out of the shelter for the night. I walked into the room where the ladies were to share with them what Masika threatened to do to me. Pretty Eyes reached into her purse and took out a hundred dollars for me to give to Masika. Pretty Eyes said that she didn't say where the money had to come from. I handed Masika that hundred dollar bill.

She told me that it was not my money and that one of the ladies just gave it to me, therefore, she was kicking me out for the night. I had less than thirty minutes to pack up my things. I went back into the room where the ladies couldn't believe that Masika was kicking me out for no good reason. I packed a bag. Pretty Eyes called her boyfriend to pick me up where the shelter van was dropping me off. I had no fear. When I got dropped off in the middle of the night at the train station, Pretty Eyes' boyfriend was waiting for me in his luxury car. He drove me to a nearby house. He got out of the car when I stayed in the car.

God reminded me that I used to work at a hotel that was nearby and He laid it upon my heart to give them a call. I called the hotel and the lady who picked up the phone was Sammy. Sammy and I used to work together at that property. We had established a relationship by going to a basketball game together and hanging out at other places. I told her all that happened to me. She told me that she so happened to have a room for the night. She was too tired to drive back home, so she was sleeping overnight at the hotel. She told me to come and share the room with her, and that I could sleep on the bed while she slept on the couch. When Pretty Eyes' boyfriend came back to the car, trying to figure out where to take me, I already had a plan. He dropped me off at the hotel, where I went straight to the hotel room and rested well in that bed. Probably the best sleep I had in a while. I woke up, took a shower, and changed my clothes. Sammy arranged for the hotel van to drop me off in town. The hotel van dropped me off near a church where I sat down while I watched a parade walking by. There was some type of festivity for a holiday that I happened to stumble upon. I didn't stay for too long as I walked to meet the shelter van.

Pretty Eyes was waiting on my arrival back at the shelter. As I headed towards the room, I noticed that Masika was in her office, so I walked in her office first. She looked like she had a rough night. She looked like what I should have looked like. Her hair was all over the place. She looked stress out. She looked a hot mess. She looked like her rest was taken. I told her how God rescued me, then I politely walked out of her office to share the testimony with Pretty Eyes. I told Pretty Eyes that I didn't have time to pray. It all happened so fast. Pretty Eyes said, "You are always praying. You were prepared for that night."

I knew that God had my back, and while I did my best, He would do what I was unable. It wasn't as if I wasn't trying. I had high hopes, but I wanted God's will to be done in my life, not my will and not anyone else's will for my life. That was my prayer.

My day to leave the shelter was coming up. The first couple of weeks seemed like the longest days of my life. But now I was flowing with what God had planned. Pretty Eyes moved out of the shelter to move into her mother's house. Her situation was not the best, as I later found out that she was living inside her mother's van parked outside her mother's house and going inside to take a shower and change clothes. Other times, I assumed that she was spending the night at her boyfriend's house.

Carol suggested that I and the other ladies go visit this church where there was a lady named Mrs. Irene, who was a volunteer. She liked to give, and when it was time to move out of the shelter, she would give us whatever we requested. One of the other ladies chimed in and said that Mrs. Irene was going to purchase her a laptop. She went on to say that Mrs. Irene and her family were wealthy. I was not interested in going to meet her. I didn't care what she was giving and how much money she had. I had been in the shelter close to ninety days and I had never gone into this church, so why would I now go? God would find another way to bless me. Besides, I felt like God was going to put me in a mansion. But again Carol kept mentioning Mrs. Irene to me for two weeks straight until I paid attention and felt like I needed to go. I felt good about my decision to go to this church to meet Mrs. Irene. And just like they said, Mrs. Irene was a sweet older woman. She was much older than I thought. She had to be in her sixties. Once I introduced myself to her, we talked about God and church. We had a lot in common.

God had to correct my motives because all I wanted was to see how she would help me. My thoughts were corrupt, so God had me to change my thought process. If anybody was going to use anyone, it would be Jesus, not me. I had to visit her because this was all about what God was doing and who He was using. Once I corrected my motives with the help of Jesus, my intentions were pure and I was able to not be tense and walk in with love and good conversation. We enjoyed each other's company. She was one of my favorite people to visit and we didn't talk about what she was giving. I told her that I was an author so she purchased thirty copies of my book and had me to autograph each copy for her family.

Masika called me into her office to go over my next moves. Masika handed me a piece of paper that had a budget for my housing and a list of places where I could rent. I had the option of renting a room or renting an apartment. I said that I wanted to rent an apartment. I would never live in a room with a whole bunch of other strange people. That would never happen. I told Pretty Eyes and she mentioned an apartment building in town that would rent to me. She told me once upon a time she tried to rent in this building, but the landlord never answered his phone, nor did he return her phone calls. She thought that I would have a better chance. So I called him and he answered. I filled out an application with the assistance paperwork and I was approved. It all happened fast, with no difficulty. I told Pretty Eyes that she could move in with me if she wanted.

The shelter had to extend my ninety days because I was taking too long to move out. I needed more time, but really I wasn't looking forward to moving again and not into an apartment. I had hopes that I was moving from the shelter into the mansion. Mrs. Irene asked me to get a list together and write down everything that I needed for my studio apartment. I needed everything down to the towels and dishes. What I put on that list, Mrs. Irene provided plus additional. She was a blessing. Pretty Eyes gave me the money for the deposit for the studio apartment. I told Pretty Eyes that at any time she needed a place to stay that she could come and live with me. I wanted her to come and live with me to continue this journey like we were in the shelter.

Pretty Eyes took me riding with her to the hair salon. She ran out of her shampoo and conditioner. I needed a new wig, and as usual, I expected her to purchase it for me as she always did. She went to pick up her items and I went to get my wig. We both stood in line while she was on her cell phone. We waited to pay when she walked out of the line and disappeared someplace, to leave me in line alone then my turn came to pay. Thank God that my mom just sent me $40 and I had $20 left. I paid for my wig and I didn't say a thing. That was a quiet ride back to the shelter. We didn't speak nor did we talk about it. I discerned in my spirit that the person she was talking to was her boyfriend. I felt like he told her that I was using her and for her to not pay for me, so she listened to him and left me hanging. I wasn't upset with her. I wanted to keep our friendship, so I didn't mention how shady that was. I really appreciated all that Pretty Eyes had done for me.

My birthday was spent living in a shelter. I turned 29 years old. The month that I was moving out of the shelter. The young lady, Isabella, who I met on our church van, handed me a gift she purchased for me. She told the van driver, Chris that her family did not approve of her going to church. She said that she had to sneak out of the house by climbing out of the window to attend Bible study. Whenever she returned home, they locked her out. I felt sorry for her and wondered what kind of family she lived with, a bunch of evil people. Isabella was sweet and five years younger than me and did not deserve that kind of treatment. I never thought that I would spend my birthday in a shelter, but here I was grateful that God had taken good care of me for so long. I had awesome people surrounding me and life could only get better. I felt like God gave me back ten years of my life.

Pretty Eyes was always going to these networking events. She met an author who was having a book signing at a fancy restaurant and she wanted me to join her. I got all dolled up in my Dress for Success outfit. As soon as we walked in, Pretty Eyes stood in line to greet her new author friend and then she turned to me to ask me right in front of the author if I wanted her to buy me a copy of her book. I didn't know what to say since she put me on the spot, but I said sure. We sat down talking to two other ladies at our table and they all ordered some food. Pretty Eyes asked me if I wanted something to eat and I told her no. She was not about to fool me twice and leave me stuck with the bill. I just sat there hungry while everybody ate around me. We talked and laughed with two other ladies sitting at our table for about two hours when one of the ladies said that she had to leave, but it was a pleasure meeting us. That night we learned that Michael Jackson had passed away, which shocked us all, and this was the topic of our conversation.

When the event was over, the waitress would not take Pretty Eyes' payment because the lady who sat at our table who left earlier paid for our meals. I was stuck like chuck. My mouth was wide open. I thought, "You mean to tell me that all of this time, I could have been eating?" I was sitting there laughing while hungry for no reason. Pretty Eyes smiled, placing her credit card back in her purse. That night I learned my lesson that God is the one blessing me and using people. God is the one in charge, not a man and He moves in the heart of man to bless His children and He will use anybody. To put your trust in God, not in man. God is doing the using.

On her own, because I came with the right intentions, Mrs. Irene started a notebook list of things that I would need going into my apartment. She covered all of my needs plus extra. There was nothing of that list short of glory. Most of the items on the list that she had for me she would have to go out and purchase. But she said that one of her friends had extra rooms in their house with beds that they did not use. She had one of her friends give me their twin bed from one of their guest rooms. Mrs. Irene was equally ecstatic to see me move out of the shelter. Giving was a part of her nature. She was wealthy and at the same time, she was a big giver. She gave to the needs of people without hesitation with a lot of love.

Pretty Eyes and the shelter had to help me see that it was time for me to move out and move on with my life. Moving out of the shelter was bittersweet for me. Yes, it was time for me to move out, and yes, it was a shelter, but this was where God placed me. I met wonderful people, even friends. I didn't want to leave anyone. I wasn't ready to move, but it was time. I went from the shelter to a furnished studio apartment. Mrs. Irene had her guys get a moving truck and move all of the new things that she had for me into my studio apartment. I had a twin size bed with all of the bedding and window curtains. Whatever I needed was there. She got me a big tall wooden table that stood across from the refrigerator and kitchen. My place was small but it was mine.

One of the men who helped me move was speaking on his cell phone and told the other person that he was doing his charity work. First of all, I took offense to that because I felt like he was calling me charity. Not even Mrs. Irene said such things about me, not around me. She always treated me with respect. Secondly, he was not telling the truth. Mrs. Irene paid him to help me and he was being rude. I didn't feel bad for him when he went to grab more items out of his truck and found a big fat parking ticket there. God always fights for His children. He should have kept his mouth shut.

The next couple of days I spent coordinating with the maintenance of my building to get a newer refrigerator because the one that he placed in my studio was old and did not work. He also had to replace my showerhead because that too was old and had mildew. I tried to get them to re-clean the bathroom, as there was black mold around the bathtub and around the bathroom tile, but all he could tell me was that the cleaner already cleaned. Well, I was not about to place my hands on that nasty filth, so I decided that it would have to stay as is since they were not going to do anything else about it. I put Clorox on it, which helped a little. I wore shower shoes whenever I showered, and I wore house shoes all day in that apartment. I placed bath rugs all on that nasty tile. I hung a maroon curtain outside the door of the bathroom so that I could keep it all hidden.

I did my best to cover the filth up with newer stuff that I purchased from Walmart. When I had enough money saved up, I went to the store to purchase Lysol, Pine sol, Clorox. I was doing deep cleaning in my apartment when my eyes started burning and getting watery. I stood outside to get some fresh air, as I was coughing and I couldn't breathe. I stood in a long dress, between my apartment building and a Jewish temple, on the side of the building a few feet from the sidewalk and main road. I liked standing there because the grounds stayed clean.

Two men were walking past me, but then they stopped when they saw me standing there. One of the men was short and ugly while the other man was attractive to the eyes. I thought that they would continue walking, but they stopped. The two men looked at each other. The taller man kept looking at me and looking out at the main road. The uglier, shorter man looked to the front of him, then to the back of him, and then to the road, like they were making sure no one was coming. It was at night and there weren't many people in the street or on the roads. Then the more attractive man placed one of his legs on a brick. I could hear the Holy Spirit telling me to move. But I ignored the Holy Spirit, because it fascinated me to watch these two men. Then the man with his leg on the brick pulled out his cell phone. I heard the Holy Spirit tell me once again to move, but I stayed. I saw the shorter uglier man open his flip phone, and for the third time, I could hear the Holy Spirit say, MOVE NOW. That time I paid attention and removed myself from the situation. I ran inside my apartment building, took the stairs to my door and went inside. I thanked God for keeping me away from harm.

Before I left the shelter, one of the ladies told me that my apartment building had mice and bed bugs and lots of roaches. I felt that she was being used by Satan to discourage me. I didn't see any bugs when I came to visit the building. I wasn't going to listen to her. This lady complained about the food in the shelter. She caused a scene once, saying that the food was nasty, complaining, and then she threw the food away in the trash. I was not going to listen to somebody like her.

A month after I moved in, Kim from the shelter moved in on the same floor, just the opposite side of the building, with her boyfriend. I thanked God that I had someone I kind of knew moving into my building since Pretty Eyes didn't move in with me. She did come to visit my new place. I told Pretty Eyes that I could place a second twin bed right beside me. Kim and I quickly became dependent on each other. She opened her apartment to me, but I came over to chill with her only a few times because she had a cat and boyfriend. She would bring me a plate of the meals she cooked, and I would braid her hair. She would give me five dollars. At night I could hear a man yelling and screaming, coming from her hallway. She told me that this man would walk the halls naked with a knife in his hand. One of the neighbors told Kim that this man was violated a long time ago and he had a mental problem. I was just glad that I didn't accept the apartment in that hall, which was the first apartment shown to me. I was glad that I was given the one that I was in on the opposite side. However, some strange men would knock on my door in the evening, speaking Spanish and looking for the previous resident. I paid it no mind. They eventually stopped knocking when I didn't answer them.

I also had this strange neighbor, Princess, who lived four doors down from me, knocking on my door. I spoke to her my first day moving in, and ever since she felt at ease to bother me. She knocked on my door, saying that her electricity was shut off and could she use my microwave to warm up her food? I opened my door to her and allowed her to warm up her food. While she sat at my brand new wood table, she started talking about Joseph from the Bible. Just talking disrespectfully about him. Now Joseph was one of my favorite people of the Bible and his story was one of the best. After she left, I said to myself that I would never let her back into my apartment. I sent Princess to Mrs. Irene and the workers of the church to help her with her electricity bill. The Catholic Church helped pay my outstanding bill before I could move in. I hoped that they would be able to help Princess. Mrs. Irene told me that Princess came to visit, but that it was all a lie. Princess had taken a black marker and marked the balance on her electricity bill. When they called the electric company, her electricity was not getting shut off. I knew that I was dealing with a crazy person. When she knocked on my door, I kept my music loud enough so she would think that I couldn't hear her. When I would go to the peephole and see her, I knew not to answer. Then she started knocking on the door, and when I went to look out my peephole, I didn't see anybody there. Until I looked one day and she appeared and looked directly back into my peephole. I would walk out of my apartment to go to the elevator, and she would rush out. Sometimes I would have my cell phone on my ear, pretending to be talking so that she wouldn't interrupt me. It worked every time.

CHAPTER FIVE

Seasons

A new season of spring has begun for my life. It had been winter far too long. Now I can see the sun. It's gratifying to have your own apartment. Even though it was small, it was mine. I would lie on my bed, envisioning Pretty Eyes lying in a twin bed next to me, being somewhat a room-mate. Her mother let her move into her house. She was doing fine, which I was happy about. Pretty Eyes was attending a ton of networking events. She invited me to a couple of them, but that was not my cup of tea. However, I supported her in what she was doing,

She organized a vision board party in an office building where they had abortions. I was confused as to why she chose that building, however, I went to support her. Only two of us showed up. Pretty Eyes had a nice setup and I learned a lot about vision boards. It was rewarding to place pictures of your dreams on a board. Pretty Eyes held her head high. While there were only two of us, it didn't seem to bother her. She moved on in fabulousness, even coor-dinating a speaking engagement in a mega church. I went with her and sat at the table with all of these speakers being treated specially. I was impressed and I felt important or at least hanging with someone who was important. I watched and listened as Pretty Eyes delivered an inspiring speech, sharing her testimony.

God was giving me new friendships. I was encouraged by all of these interesting friendships that God placed in my life. I was surrounded by love and felt taken care of. Chris became more than the church van driver, he became my friend. He was the only person from my church who invited me to different church members' gatherings at their houses. If it was not for Chris, I would not know half the people from my church. He not only invited me, but he came to pick me up from my apartment and drop me off. No one beside him initiated the love and support beyond what they were supposed to do. I saw Chris like a brother. He would take me on hikes where we talked about his separation from his wife, from his fourth marriage. I shared how God helped me deal with the ending of my marriage. That process hurt me so bad that I wouldn't wish that kind of pain on my worst enemy.

Chris was proud of the fact that I published my first book and was working on publishing my second book in my struggles. I could tell that he was proud because, after he introduced me to people, he always told them I was an author. We had a few things in common and I could relate to not having your own place living with other people. When he moved out of the home that he shared with his wife, he moved into the basement of one of the couples from our church. It was a finished basement that was charming. He had a cozy set up. He would pick me up to spend time with them to eat home-cooked meals. He also had me to sing backup with him after he found out that I could sing. I would come over his house for evening practice to practice in his basement room along with the couple. That was a good time.

Some of the women from our church rolled their eyes at me when they saw how close Chris and I were. But they did not understand the dynamics of our relationship. Besides, not one of them invited me over to their houses for lunch or dinner. No one asked me how I was doing. So to tell you the truth, I didn't care, because God didn't need their permission for what He put together. This was a God blessing and

I wouldn't allow anyone to interfere with the blessings that I always received.

Not only was Chris married, but he was a much older man. I couldn't tell how old he was with his clean bald head. Chris was clean in how he took care of himself, from his outfits to his clean car and basement room, and had a spunky attitude that matched mine. I was surprised when he revealed his age, fifty-four years old. He didn't look a day over thirty-five. He was young in heart and that manifested in his demeanor. He was always a man on the go and I enjoyed his company very much. Now that did not mean that Chris didn't flirt with me at the beginning of our relationship because he sure did. I shut down his subtle flirtatious ways at the start. It can become confusing when you spend quality time with the opposite sex. Which is why I continued to pray because if not then we could have mistaken our friendship for something more.

Now that my circle was solid if I wasn't with Chris or Pretty Eyes, I was hanging out with Carlos. Carlos was still living in the shelter, but he found a job at the donut shop and was looking for a new place to live. He was up for a promotion, which I had to coach him to take. He shared with me his fears of taking the promotion. He said in his past when he lived in the 'hood, he was up for a similar promotion but didn't take it because his peers made fun of him and told him that he couldn't do it. So he went back to selling drugs. I told him that he was more than capable of being a boss and he was no longer in the 'hood. He could do it. I kind of missed Carlos. When I lived in the shelter, sometimes he would purposely sit next to me during dinner whenever I came down for the second platter. He would scoot my seat next to him and sing Michael Jackson's song, Pretty Young Thing. That was the first time I heard about that song, through him.

Carlos came to visit my new place to see how it looked and to play catch up. I met him downstairs, and as we were headed to my apartment, he made a comment that I moved into the 'hood. I smiled and dismissed what he had to say because I didn't see the ghetto. He entered my apartment and he was impressed with what Mrs. Irene blessed me with. I told him that whenever it was time for him to move out that Mrs. Irene could do the same for him. Mrs. Irene told me to share this information with others. I was selective in who I told that to, but Carlos was one of those special people who I made sure to tell what Mrs. Irene could do. He sat on my bed while I sat on my stool, talking, but then we got interrupted by my neighbor Princess's knock. I didn't answer her, but she yelled that she needed help with hooking up her cable. Although she played me once before, I looked at Carlos as to ask if he would be willing to help. Carlos looked back at me, and with a stern, "No," we proceeded to continue our conversation as it was before we got interrupted. I moved to sit next to him on the bed to keep talking. That was when he leaned in for a kiss. Now, I was a passionate kisser, and at the moment he took his hand and lifted up my shirt.

I stopped kissing to see his eyes staring at my shirt where half of my boob was exposed. But I felt like this could not be me right now. We stopped kissing and I put my shirt down. We talked for a little while longer and then he had to leave to be someplace else. I was in deep thought as we walked outside my apartment building that I was not the girl who could give him what he was looking for. No matter how many times I tried telling him now I had to show him that I was a Christian girl on a path. Not that it would make a difference as I had pretty much shown him during the duration of our friendship. I was conflicted with my emotions towards Carlos. He wouldn't change his behavior towards me because he had a different thought process than mines. He didn't want to be holy. He made that clear to me yet I still considered being his girlfriend after I moved out the shelter. But I never told him and I didn't invite him back to my apartment. I figured, no more alone time. I asked God to forgive me because I put myself in a compromising position.

I was diligently looking for work daily and completing the process of publishing my second book. I went back to the same publisher that published my first book, but they didn't like the title of my book that the Lord gave to me, which was LIFE. They changed my title without my permission and added a cover for the book that looked fake. I was about to take them to court just to get my rights back. I met a gentleman who was a paralegal who assisted me for free in drawing up motions to execute the court process. My publishing company called me all sorts of names and made it seem like I was a liar and a lulu bird. But I stood my ground and we settled the case out of court. They released my book back to me which is all that I wanted.

I took a break to process the thoughts of self-publishing. I figured this was the route for me since I wanted to keep the title of my book and the content could not change. I needed more control. But self-publishing would cost me money that I was not ready for, so I placed the publishing process on hold. I still looked for work by sending out hundreds of emails. As I sat in the Workforce building, I could see several women and men coming in to file for their unemployment. The women usually entered the room in tears while the men held it in. However, I could tell that they were torn apart. The saddest thing was to see a man distraught. I prayed for some of the people. Once I was evangelizing to one of the people at Workforce when that person made it perfectly clear that he was not interested in what I had to say. I was about to give up hope on ministering to folks. I felt like, "Why do I waste my time?" and that was when I heard a voice tell me not to give up. It was another person listening in on the conversation. They told me to keep ministering and never shut up. It goes to show that you never know whose listening.

Following the Workforce, I sat at the Greene, a park in my town, to write. Sitting down on the bench among the trees with the breeze, a squirrel showed up beside my feet, making hissing noises. I decided to relocate to another bench. That was when I noticed the squirrel seemed like he followed me. I tried to ignore his annoying hissing sound. Subsequently, a Rasta with dreadlocks, with a Bob Marley t-shirt came to introduce himself to me, then he sat down next to me. He told me that he was driving past the park when he saw me. He told me that it was not a good idea for me to be hanging out in the park all of the time. Some of the people were not like me. It was not always safe. He spoke his words and then he departed. That's when I heard a voice in the distance. It was a young man who stayed in the shelter at the same time as me, with his girlfriend. They didn't stay long. I heard that they got kicked out for drugs. He was motioning for me to come to him. I also noticed two random men standing next to him, looking in my direction. I saw these men walking around town in black trench coats. They dressed in all black. These two men looked as if they were up to no good. Well, this man kept calling for me, and I knew it was time for me to leave. I packed up my stuff and scooted up out of that park. I appreciated that Rasta for coming and speaking truth to me. He didn't know that I had decided to make the park my spot to hang out. Now I would find another place that was safe. I would only be in that park if it served a purpose, and prefer-ably not being by myself.

Appreciating my studio apartment, I walked fifteen min-utes to the closest grocery store to buy food to cook. I must admit that it felt good to be able to cook for myself, having my own space. It was usually packaged meals. Nonetheless, it was my time and how I wanted it. I had a few of my friends from the shelter come to visit me. Mainly Pretty Eyes came to visit. At times I gave Pretty Eyes my food stamp card since she was living with her family. Her unemployment ran out and she had no money saved. She spent $400 on an Apple iPhone. I thought that was foolish spending, but Pretty Eyes had a different agenda. I gave her my card so that she could have something to contribute to her family's household in hopes that they would not put her out. Besides, she had done so much for me that I wanted to give back in some way, even if she didn't ask, which she didn't. Her man gave her money from time to time.

Kim came over for me to braid her hair when I finished and she walked home. I sat down to relax when the biggest cockroach came crawling from the outside hall into the open space of my front door, right into my apartment. I was livid and I screamed. The last time I saw a roach was when I was a teen at somebody else's house. Not even the shelter had roaches. This was crazy and all that I could handle. I fell asleep in my stress. A part of me was trying to monitor the door. I was awakened when God lifted my arm to reposition it. I guess I was sleeping on it wrong. God knew that if He didn't do that, I would have awakened in more pain. When the morning came, I didn't want to get up, so I felt God's hand smack me so hard that I jumped up and got dressed. As soon as I had my clothes, on Pretty Eyes knocked on my door unannounced. We headed out. To my surprise, she treated me to groceries and a free movie. She couldn't even stay in the theater for too long because she was dozing off to sleep. I ended up watching the movie alone. This was just what my mind and soul needed.

I knew the steps of being on housing assistance. After the shelter, I was supposed to partake in volunteering. It took the place of having a job, so you volunteer until you find employment. But no one called me to transition. My new counselor, Steve, who was over the volunteers, told me that I would be starting a mandatory class where I had to create new resumes before sending them out for successful results. I spent half of the day in this mandatory class. The other half of the day I had to spend looking for work. I had to log my hours, also what I did in those hours, including my contacts, dates, and times. Of course, I couldn't be in the class but for a split second before I experienced unnecessary drama from my instructor. Of course, Satan would use the ones closest to me to try to distract and discourage me. You would think that I did something awful to this woman, the way she came for me every day of class. It bothered me, but I had to keep my lips closed because of the moment that I became a problem,

I could lose my assistance. The slightest wrong move and I could be sanctioned.

I was wise with the help of the Lord. Plus I've learned that God will fight my battles and He can do a much better job than I could ever do. As I was finalizing my resume, my instructor reviewed it and came up with the conclusion that I needed to delete my education where I mentioned biblical studies. She said that no employer wanted to see that, so it would be hard for me to find a job. She also said that biblical studies had nothing to do with a job. Out of respect for her and my position, I deleted it from my resume. But when I got home, I rethought about it and came up with my own conclusion. I talked with God about this situation. I told God that if a job didn't want to hire me because I had biblical studies as my education, then that was not the job for me. Also when the instructor told me that biblical studies had nothing to do with a job, I thought that was a lie from the devil himself. Anyone who hired me would know that they were hiring someone with morals, integrity, love, compassion, and a hard worker because they knew that I had God to answer to.

When I went back to class, I wrote my education back onto my resume. The instructor looked at me with an evil eye, but I didn't care. Her part was to give me direction and advice, and it was up to me if I took it, and she was supposed to respect my choice. It was my resume.

Olivia's ex-husband called me out of the blue to see if I could come to Maryland for a week to help watch his teenage daughters. He accepted a new position that required him to travel for work. Since he just relocated, he didn't trust anyone to be there for his children. I had watched his daughters when they were babies. I was the only one that he felt comfortable with, and he knew that I was not working. I was just a few hours' drives away. I was hopeful when he presented this opportunity to me. I needed to get away from my world, if just for a moment. I would take it. His kids were old enough for this time away to be exciting and fun, I presented a letter to my counselor, Steve, who granted me leave to go and watch the kids. God was good in rescuing me out of the hands of the enemy. I promise you that tension was hot, but God reached down and pulled me out.

Olivia's ex-husband drove down to pick me up just a couple of days after asking me to come. The girls and I had a blast when he went out of town for work. They were recovering from the divorce of their parents. Their father left us his truck and money so that we could have a good time. We went to the zoo, restaurants, driving around and enjoying each other's company. We prayed together and we cooked a nice home-cooked meal. I felt relaxed and mentally I was strong. When I returned back home, I was ready for whatever task God had for me to do.

Immediately upon my return to New Jersey, Steve had arranged for me to interview for volunteer work with a couple of office managers at different locations throughout Morris County. They weren't walking distance, therefore, I had to take the bus to travel to and from, walking up hills and through fields of grass to catch the bus. There were random people, both women, and men, stopping to try to give me a ride. They all said that I looked like I needed help. I declined their offer but I was tired. I went to God to ask Him where should I volunteer? Where's the best place to be? There was an office position available for a volunteer at the daycare center walking distance from my apartment. I thought this would be great, so I went for an interview on a Friday. I hurried up to tell Steve that I wanted to take the volunteer office assistant position at the daycare center. Steve wanted to expedite the paperwork Monday morning. I had a nice weekend and when Monday rolled around Steve had disappointing news for me. He told me that the position was given to someone else. I kept asking him to see if they had another office position available, where I could come and help. They did not have any office work but they did have volunteer openings working with the children. While I had no aspirations to work with little children I felt like that place was where God was leading me. Steve tried to figure out where else to send me to interview and sell me on the others that I went to previously. Those office managers that I interviewed for were very interested in me coming back to their office to volunteer. Those managers were impressed with my typing skills and that I was able to take direction. I went back to God and asked Him where should I volunteer and please give me a sign of where to go.

I rode past this particular daycare when Pretty Eyes' son came walking out. I took this as a sign. I asked God again to show me a sign, and again God showed me when another familiar person who came walking out of that daycare center. I knew in my heart that was where God was leading me, no matter how it didn't add up or what it looked like. Steve tried to talk me out of it. He even offered a position in his building to help out, but I was settled in my heart for the daycare center. My only request was that they did not place me in a room with infants. I wasn't able to handle that. Steve had to accept my decision and reluctantly began the paperwork. I had no idea how this would go, but I had peace in my heart.

I met with the Director of the daycare center to begin the process of becoming a volunteer. I took a drug test and a background check. I had a couple of weeks of downtime before I was to start my volunteer work at the daycare center. I never thought that I would ever work with children. I had some experience with children watching my best friend's kids. When I was younger, my mom had me to watch her friends' children when they went out on the town, and I always watched my siblings when my mother went to work or was hanging out with her friends, so being around children was not foreign to me. But working at a daycare center was a whole new arena for me. Nothing thus far had made sense, however, I had to believe that it all served a purpose, Jeremiah 29:11, "For I know the thoughts that I think toward you, saith the Lord, thoughts of peace, and not of evil, to give you an expected end." God scriptures, has kept me humbled and moving forward in strength and confidence in Jesus.

God Made Me to Be a Soldier

Back at my apartment building the fire alarm was going off every night. When I first moved in, I was running out no matter the time so that I could be someplace safe, but after the twentieth time, I didn't bother going out. I just hoped that it would never be a for real fire. I thought someone was playing some twisted joke that had the firemen coming out all of the time. I was in and out, not talking to anyone but speaking to some of the men on the first floor who had their doors open every weekend as they hosted a party. Whenever I walked by, they all were sitting by the door, enjoying loud music, drugs, and playing cards. The two men always spoke and I spoke back but I never interacted with them or their company.

Kim, my neighbor, still came to my apartment to get her hair braided. She would give me a couple of dollars. It was never a lot of money but it was something. I was proud of her success as a recovered addict. She went to work and never missed a day. She showed up to drug court sober and she lived in an apartment with her boyfriend, who later became her fiancé. To celebrate her milestone, I accompanied her to one of her AA meetings that her fiancé attended too, just to show my support. She laid down the rules to me before we got there. The AA meetings were held in a church in our town where we lived. She told me that it was all secret. I couldn't share what they talked about and I couldn't tell who was in the meeting. I saw a few people who I recognized from the shelter. But to be there among the people was rewarding for me. They were brave to overcome an addiction and be free to express their story. I admired their journey and process. Even though I didn't believe in living with someone before marriage, to me, Kim was headed in the right direction and I was exceedingly happy for her life moving forward in a positive direction.

My place was beginning to be a hectic way of living. It wasn't like this at first. God didn't allow me to see the crazy, but the crazy was recognizable after six months of being a tenant. These roaches crawling up my wall were disgusting. They were few and far between and small when they came out of hiding to crawl up my wall. I hated bugs. I never had them before. Not even the shelter had them, so this was unsettling. I wanted to get bug spray but I feared that the moment I sprayed they would sense it and it would attract more of them to come out. While the purpose was to kill them, I just wanted them to stay in hiding wherever the heck they were at. Later I asked the maintenance man to make sure the exterminator came to my apartment. I came to find out the exterminator was due at our apartment building twice a month. Whoever was not in their apartment upon their arrival, their apartment did not get exterminated. Well, no one told me about this before, so I made sure that I was at home every time the exterminator came. As they said, he did come twice a month, and this seemed to help with the bug problems, so I thought.

Just when I was getting comfortable, I heard mice in the walls, but I never saw them. When it was completely silent, I could hear them scratching in the walls, so I purposely had my radio on every night set on the Christian radio station. I couldn't hear them any longer, but just as I was getting relaxed again, I heard a mouse walking on the side of my wall a few inches from my bed. I couldn't believe my life, but still, I had to handle this. I'm telling you, God made me to be a soldier because before Christ I would have packed my bags and moved back home to my mother, ASAP. I screamed when I heard that mouse running against my wall.

The maintenance man told me that if I purchased the mice traps that snapped, then I would see their blood, so this didn't sound like anything I was interested in seeing. He suggested another option that I could place sticky pads that would catch them, but they would still be alive and I could hear them, but they would be stuck on that mouse pad. This was a better option for me so I went and purchased a few traps to hold me until the maintenance man received his order of mice traps. He said that he would place more down for me. This mouse situation was taking a toll on me. Whenever I went outside and the wind blew the leaves on the ground, I would jump. I placed mice traps all around the walls. I could hear them coming out at night and sure enough, they were on my traps still alive. I took a hanger and bagged them in a garbage bag and took them down to our basement trash room, sometimes at 2 am.

The maintenance man brought a ton of mice traps to place them throughout my apartment in hiding places where I couldn't see them. He placed them under the refrigerator, stove, under the bathroom sink that had this huge opening, and under my dressers. Also, the maintenance man covered the bottom of my front door with weather-strip. There was a reasonable gap between the floor and the bottom of my door that allowed these little critters to enter. I was having it rough at my studio apartment. I decided to never cook by using the stove or oven in my apartment again. I would only use the microwave from time to time. I later learned that the daycare center cooked food for the children, so there was my lunch. A few weeks into volunteering, they hired this professional chef who made the babies' lunches. We went from having frozen chicken strips to chicken parmesan. You would think that you were sitting down in a restaurant instead of a daycare center. I'm telling you, favor followed me everywhere I stepped in.

I grew to love being around the children. They brought a sense of peace and calm, pure joy, and laughter that kept me from breaking down. It's an honor to be in their presence. It brought a balance in my hectic world. I was passionate about my role as a volunteer. Some of the hired teachers' assistants became jealous of me, whispering about me in the distance, but I kept handling my responsibilities. They weren't rude to me directly, because I was submissive, but I observed and kept my distance. I knew that my time there was temporary. I was happy that God led me to work at the daycare. I volunteered four hours a day with the weekends off. It was down the street from my apartment. I was off on holidays and any days the school was off, and this establishment was more flexible with my call outs whenever I was sick or just wanted some "me" time. If I had volunteered at the office jobs where everyone else preferred that I worked, this would have been a lot of tension and a strain on my mind and body. I was glad that God took over my life and steered me in the right direction. A place that was calmer and willing to work with my schedule, if need be. All around, this was the best decision.

When my four hours of volunteering was complete. I had to go and sign into the Workforce to look for work for the remaining of the day. There I met Christina, an older black woman who was constantly at the Workforce computer looking for work. She always wore long summer dresses with sandals. She had long black hair and she was roughly ten years older than me. God was placing all these older people in my life. Isabella was the only one who was younger than me. Christina and I sat near each other while searching for work on computers. She told me that she was working but lost her two jobs. She also shared with me that her sister worked at the headquarters of Victoria's Secret and she received free perfumes and body lotion. The next day she brought me a bag full of perfumes and lotions. I wasn't the freshest person to smell, so I was eager to dive right into these smell goods. This made my day. Proverbs 27:9, "Ointment and perfume rejoice the heart: so doth the sweetness of a man's friend by hearty counsel."

When Christina and I talked, I learned that she was no longer a Christian. She used to attend a Christian church, but she became uninterested when the church members were gossiping and doing everything that they were not supposed to do. They were being messy and hypocrites and causing a lot of strife. She didn't have any peace. She met someone who introduced her to a guru. This guru was all about peace and love. I, of course, didn't believe in what she was doing, but I kept quiet. I knew there would be a time when I would tell her about Jesus, but now it was important for me to show her that not all believers of Jesus Christ were hypocrites and causing strife and were loud and obnoxious. She invited me over to her house and she cooked me meals and introduced me to her lovely, tall and beautiful daughter.

God presented an opportunity through one of the teachers I became close with, who invited me to attend her church. It was a Spanish church inside of a movie theater. They had a Spanish side and an English side. She was a child of God and we talked about God and how He was blessing our lives. We took care of each other in class. She had some of the parents tip me money when they had a party at the kids' daycare with the parents and their children. This money was helpful. I never took that kind of blessings for granted. She told me that her church was having a baptism. I never got baptized by water because my grandmother put the fear of God in me. My grandmother told us a scary story when we were kids about a boy who went to get baptized and almost drowned. She told us to take getting baptized seriously. Well, I never wanted to get baptized by water until I was serious about my journey with the Lord. My church held a baptism and I attended the classes until I lost my car, then my world was flipped upside down and I could no longer attend the baptism classes, therefore, I never got baptized. This teacher told me that her pastor was having a baptism, and although I was not a member of their church, I could still come. I just had to answer some of the questions that they had. Her two pastors met me at a local diner to go over the meaning of baptism and had me to answer a few questions. When we were done, they invited me to come over the weekend to one of their members' house, where the baptism would be held. The church member's house had a big pool.

That weekend came and it was special. There was a huge gathering of people preparing to get baptized. I wanted this moment to be special, so I came all natural, leaving my wig at home. My turn came to get baptized and it began to pour down rain. The two pastors prayed for me and on both sides of me dipped me in the water. I already had it in my mind to stay down a little longer. I had no desire for this to be quick. I was not about to get dipped and brought back up so fast. So when the two pastors said their prayer and dipped me, I stayed down much longer. The two pastors had to put some muscle in their arms to push me back up. When I got up it was incredible. Some of the people came up to me to tell me that my baptism was amazing and they wondered if I was going to come back up.

Shortly after the baptism, Olivia's ex-husband called me once again to ask if I could come to Maryland to watch his kids while he traveled for work. Steve approved it however the head teacher became angry at me even causing a stir, but I went away anyway. My Christian teacher at the day-care center was the only one that was supportive. The head teacher acted as if I actually worked for their company like they could make the decision, but reality set in for her that I was not on the payroll. I went on my trip to Maryland and had a blessed time. A time to get refreshed, and rejuvenated. One of the first things I did when I arrived in their house was take a bath. I hadn't taken a bath in over a year so I knew that I would leave a ring around the tub. I had to disinfect and scrub that tub hard to get it back clean, but it was all worth it. Taking a bath is something that I looked forward to immensely. When the kid's father arrived back home after our long week of adventure, he let me keep the money that we had left over plus he treated us to dinner at a restaurant.

When I returned to New Jersey I was in a state of being content. I could endure the hardships like a champion because I knew that God had me. My phone rang and it was my mother on the other end telling me that my Grandmother Iris had passed. I knew of my Grandmother's health issues but I didn't think that she would pass away what seemed to be suddenly. God gave me solace when my mother said that my Grandmother passed away with a smile on her face. I believe that God must've visited her. Instead of joining my family for the funeral I decided to stay in New Jersey and have my own memorial service. I knew in my heart that I gave my Grandmother her roses while she was here on earth. I was also upset with a lot of extended family members and my Grandmother's friends who never paid her a visit when she lived in the nursing home nor when she was living with her brother. I had a lot of resentment inside of me towards those people. It was best that I stayed in New Jersey.

I walked to a local dollar store to purchase a bag of colorful balloons and I blew them up with my mouth to let them go up in the air at the park. The problem was that when I got to the park, the balloons didn't fly away. They stayed on the ground, which was terribly disappointing. I couldn't figure it out until Olivia came to visit me a few days after receiving the unfortunate news of my Grandmother. She told me with laughter that I should have used helium.

Olivia came to New York with her boyfriend for their trip. This was the first time that I met her new boyfriend and he wasn't pleasant to be around. He rubbed me the wrong way the moment they picked me up from my apartment. Olivia took me to her new boyfriend's Caribbean festival in New York. The next night she came to pick me up alone and left her boyfriend at the hotel with his friends and family. Olivia came into my apartment. She wouldn't even go inside my bathroom. She went inside and came right back out. She changed clothes right in front of me and washed up in my kitchen sink. When we walked out of my apartment to take the stairs, there was this drunk man sleeping. She took my hands and we turned around to take the elevator.

She was not impressed with my life and seemed to be confused. This didn't stop us from having a good time together during our night out. I went to my first Broadway show in New York City. She fell asleep, but I loved that occasion. Olivia taught me to turn the other way when we saw that man sleeping on my stairs in my building. God gave me this scripture, Proverbs 4:14 &15, "Enter not into the path of the wicked and go not in the way of evil men. Avoid it, pass not by it, turn from it, and pass away." My best friend didn't go to church yet she taught me that night.

A short time after her visit, I lay in my bed at night and got up to use the bathroom, but I heard the Holy Spirit tell me not to move. I had the covers in my mouth as I watched a gang of mice running in and out of my bathroom. This was the scariest thing that I ever saw. There were so many running in and out, it was terrifying. All I could do was grab my covers over my mouth and body, screaming and in complete shock. I didn't use the bathroom at all that night and it was hard for me to fall asleep, but I managed to go to sleep. I woke up not happy about my situation. I contacted my maintenance guy, who placed a lot of mice traps underneath my bathroom sink and underneath my refrigerator. He also closed up some holes in my closet. That explained why my clothes always had this nasty odor. I took very few showers and utilized my kitchen sink to wash up.

Chris came to pick up Isabella and myself to have Thanksgiving at his house. We ate fish with the head on it. The family who Chris was renting their basement was born in a different country, they incorporated some of their family traditions with the American Thanksgiving. I have to say, eating food with other people from different cultures is eye-opening. Some food I refused to eat. I liked to keep it simple. Just give me the turkey and potatoes. It was tasty. I was appreciative to have friends from my church who opened their homes to us for the holiday. This meant so much.

They had a karaoke machine, where we song until 2 am. Isabella and I drank grape cider, pretending that we were drinking wine out of the bottle, totally acting silly. We enjoyed ourselves so much at their house. I ended up spending the night at Isabella's house. For Christmas, Isabella invited me to spend the holiday with her family. She was visiting a new church that held their services inside of a hotel. For Christmas, they had arranged for a photographer who took our pictures in front of the massive, decorated Christmas tree. As we entered the sanctuary, the greeters handed us candles. We sang Christmas songs with the lights off, holding the candles. It was spectacular and something that I would never forget. Isabella and I took a picture together that she later hung up in her bedroom. When I came to visit her, there the picture stood against her dresser.

In the winter, I found a bar that was having a grand opening, and as part of their opening, they were serving complimentary pasta meals with salad and sometimes chicken every Thursday starting at 4 pm. Once I got a hold of this information, I was there every week at 4 pm before the bar got crowded. They also had sit-down table areas. Some days I sat at the bar if I was in a hurry. The only thing that I needed to buy was something to drink, and that wasn't mandatory. I figured that if I was going to enter their establishment and eat their food, I should at least buy something to drink. I ordered a soft drink, a lemonade. I began inviting some of the girls to eat with me. A few times, Pretty Eyes came and then Christina. Isabella came once when I invited them all at the same time to eat for free with me. We all sat at the table together when Isabella whispered in my ear that she was uncomfortable. I excused myself and told the other two ladies that Isabella and I were leaving. Isabella and I walked to her house. Although she was young in age, she was mature for her age. Her sister said that I looked like her age and Isabella looked like my age. This would upset Isabella, but I found it comical. I began to spend the night at Isabella's house. Her mom would wake us up with breakfast served with a side of white rice. I didn't know what her mother put in that rice, but it came out tasty every time. I learned many things hanging out with Isabella and Pretty Eyes. Besides the fact that they were soft-spoken and ladies with few words. We didn't fight over foolish things. We were all trying to live life for Christ.

Isabella and Pretty Eyes strengthened me in ways I couldn't imagine. I started to emulate them in areas that improved my behavior. When they spoke it was softly and they didn't talk too much. When I ate at Isabella's house, they served the food in smaller portions. I use to eat like a man but that all changed when I began to eat dinner at Isabella's house. I learned to pace myself, speak softly and that I didn't always have to have something to say. I learned how to listen. These ladies friendship played a significant role in my life. I appreciated God for placing these ladies in my world. I knew that we had a solid friendship that would last forever.

Stay In Faith

We entered a new year, 2010, with a positive attitude about life. I was continuing to look for work and volunteering at the daycare center. Along with looking for work, I was working on publishing my second book and then I began to sing backup for Chris and the married couple he lived with. They traveled to different churches singing Christian songs. Every week, Chris was picking me up for practice and dropping me back off at home.

Thank God that I got to hang out with Chris and his friends. I never told my friends that these were the times that I got to eat a meal most days. In the back of my mind, while I searched for a job, I was reminded that God had the best job for me and He would present it to me at the perfect time. One that would pay me enough money to pay my bills and still have enough money to have fun. A job that would make sense for my travel, since I didn't have a car. I waited patiently and prayed to God to help me with my faith. I wasn't in a rush to jump into anything. I was waiting on Jesus' blessing that would arrive on time.

Since I was sharing my food stamp card with Pretty Eyes, I ran out of food in my apartment to include I wasn't cooking. I was only using my microwave to warm up food, but I ran out of that quick since I only used my freezer, not my refrigerator, which stayed empty. I didn't use the refrigerator part because it was too close to the ground and it didn't make me feel at ease to store my food in there. As a result of my discomfort, I kept my snacks and drinks sitting on top of the high table that was across from my bed.

I ate my last snack and had no meals, nor did anyone invite me to their house this time to eat. I didn't panic. Instead, I walked out of my apartment building in faith. I walked a couple of blocks when I saw this dark-skinned guy who I recognized as the gentleman who worked as a van driver for a company, picking up passengers from the train station to drop them off at the hotel. He used to flirt with me while I waited for the shelter van. I didn't pay him any mind, although he was nice and attractive. He thought that I was a Muslim woman one night because I had a scarf covering my head and part of my face. It was the dead of winter and raining so I was working on trying to not get my wig wet. I later found out that he was a Muslim. Well, this day that I ran out of food, he pulled up beside me in his car. He politely ordered me, with a smile on his face, to come with him to have dinner at a restaurant I chose. I recognized this was a blessing sent from Jesus to feed me. I didn't hesitate to get into his car and he drove us to my favorite IHOP restaurant in Newark. A restaurant that Santrese and I used to hang out in when I was staying with her. I ordered a steak, rice, and veggie platter. When we finished eating he dropped me back off at my apartment not to be heard of again.

On a sunny day soon after this gentleman treated me to dinner in Newark, I had one can of soda in hand, walking down the street, not worried about how I was going to quench my thirst. I just walked in faith. I knew that God would supply my needs according to His riches and glory. I walked towards the cafe with the intentions to bypass it. This cafe was the place where I had my soup and hot tea when I lived in the shelter. To my dismay they were going out of business. They had carts full of beverages, mainly juices in glass bottles. The owner gave me permission to take as much as my heart desired. I walked away with so much that I had enough to share. I walked to Pretty Eyes' house to share my testimony and offer her a few bottles that she happily took. God was amazing in fulfilling my every need and providing provisions. I say that God sent me manna from heaven. Even days I would walk out of my apartment and take the stairs, I'd find $20 lying on the steps. Many days this saved me from starving.

I still didn't have much money and my mother was no longer sending me the monthly money. She even stopped paying my cell phone, so I had to get a government phone that I lost the first week of having it. I last saw it when I was with the children, but the phone was small and thin. It probably fell out of my pocket and I didn't hear it. I had no phone to call people. I had to go to the Workforce to check my messages and make phone calls to jobs to set up interviews. I've been strong for so long but as the struggle continued for as long as it did I became weary. I didn't see my life changing as quickly as I hoped. I thought by this time I would be in a mansion instead of a bug-infested studio apartment. I tried hard to not complain out of fear that my life would end up like the Israelites so I kept my mouth shut but this didn't stop me from thinking. I wondered where was my life going? My life should have changed big time by now. I found it easier for me to simply fall asleep than to deal with the memories of all the ups and downs that I have experienced.

I kept my radio station locked on the Gospel and Christian music. Every day I heard messages about "your blessing is around the corner," "God is an on-time God," "God will bless you," and "I have never seen the righteous forsaken." I thought that sounded good. I heard the Holy Spirit respond by saying, "It is good." After hearing God respond to my thought, it let me know that He was still there, taking care of me, and it was all good. I have testimony on top of the testimony of how good and loyal God has been to me. All I could do was to stay positive and stay in faith. Fight the good fight of faith like one of God's disciples: 2 Peter 3:9, "The Lord is not slack concerning his promise, as some men count slackness; but is longsuffering to us-ward, not willing that any should perish, but that all should come to repentance." And

Matthew 6:31&34, "Therefore take no thought saying, What shall we eat? Or, What shall we drink? Or, Wherewithal shall we be clothed? (For after all these things do the Gentiles seek:) for your heavenly Father knoweth that ye have need of all these things. But seek ye first the kingdom of God, and his righteousness, and all these things shall be added unto you. Take therefore no thought for the morrow: for the morrow shall take thought for the things of itself. Sufficient unto the day is the evil thereof."

At Workforce, I met a man by the name of Tom. He was on housing assistance looking for work. He lived in one of the hotels where I heard that they have bedbugs, roaches, and not that well clean. Not a place for anyone to be living, nor a place I thought that assisted living would send anyone however Tom was there and they sent him there to live. Tom's clothes looked run down and old, but he was a happy camper every day. He was a positive human who had positive things to say. He talked about knowing God, and then in the next breath, he shared how he looks for food in the garbage can. He seemed to be content with this, yet this revelation bothered me. I told him that he didn't have to eat food out of the trash can. I judged him and questioned within myself if he truly believed in God. Here I was having faith for steak meals and I was eating that, and here he was eating food from the trash can and we both prayed to the same God. This didn't make sense to me, but then I went home, read the Bible, my fingers turned to Romans 14:1-3, "Him that is weak in the faith receive ye, but not to doubtful disputations. For one believeth that he may eat all things: another, who is weak eateth herbs. Let not him that eateth despise him that eateth not; and let not him which eateth not judge him that eateth: for God hath received him." From that moment on, I believed that Tom and I prayed to the same God and that He was a Believer of JESUS CHRIST.

Chris called me to invite me to go with him to Ocean Grove beach. He let me know that all I needed to do was bring myself while he took care of the rest. Chris prepared for us tasty sandwiches, fruits, plenty of snacks, and water. When we arrived at the beach, I fell asleep on a blanket under the sun, listening to the waters. When I woke up, Chris was sitting on his beach chair, reading a book. I must've slept for over an hour. When I woke up we walked the boardwalk to get ice cream. As we walked I noticed these little huts that intrigued me. One of the people invited us inside their small bungalow after I asked. It intrigued me because it was small like how could anyone live in one of these but once we went in, it was a reasonable size. My soul was satisfied as we sat on the beach looking out into the ocean. Then Chris and I saw dolphins swimming by in the distance doing flips in the water entertaining us. The best way to end our summer.

CHAPTER SIX

The God of Miracles

I am blessed to have a friend like Chris a male figure in my life. Someone who doesn't mind spending time with me in a respectable manner. Chris has been such a gentleman and such a caring person to go out of his way to invite me to so many different places, come pick me up and drop me back off at my apartment every weekend and every holiday. I am never alone. Spending time with Chris lets me know that I need to be treated with love and kindness. Whenever Chris and I would spend time together we always talked about God's very best for our lives that included our future mates. Chris was thinking about reconciling with his estranged wife and I was just wondering when would God bring my Boaz? God was taking a mighty long time and I was beginning to lose my patience. I had been single and celibate for over a year. I wasn't in a position to be in a serious, committed relationship but I was down with hanging out and going on a couple of dates. No harm in that. Carlos was no Boaz but he was standing in front of me about my age, handsome, charming, witty, and single. His flirtatious ways had me to consider him to be more than a friend possibly a boyfriend. I didn't share this with Carlos. I kept it to myself to see how he would treat me even after that situation. I figured that he learned his lesson.

Carlos asked me to go to the beach with him and to his surprise, I said yes. We set a day and time that we would meet up in town to head off to the beach. I didn't tell Carlos but secretly I was anticipating a good time hanging out with him. I went shopping for a new bathing suit with a beach bag. Carlos was going to take the shelter van into town and we were going to meet up and head to the beach. Not sure how we were getting there but I was all for it. When the day had come I waited for Carlos until the evening and he never showed up nor answered my phone calls when I called him and left him numerous messages with his friends at the shelter. I was totally confused at Carlos. How could you ask me to hang out with you and you don't show up? To me, Carlos didn't give me the impression that he would not show up as he's always been there for me but this time he didn't even answer my phone calls. It was strange but I took it as a sign that maybe this was not the right time for us to be hanging out at beaches and thangs. I still was curious about seeing our relationship blossom.

God blessed Carlos to move out of the shelter into his own apartment in an area that I once wished that I lived in. Carlos asked me a couple of times to come over to his apartment. As a friend, I was proud of Carlos and how far he had come. I never wanted him to go back to the life that he once lived that landed him in prison. He needed to stay being free and I was there to stand in the gap for him. I felt like it was his season to blossom.

I made it clear to Carlos that when I come to visit him that I wouldn't have money to take the train ride back into town. Carlos offered to pay pulling out rolls of money out of his pants pockets. Carlos met me at the train station when I arrived in his town which is a clean, quiet, and adorable town. When you walk up to his apartment it seems like it's built inside a house with a whole bunch of small apartments built in it. I liked that Carlos apartment had its own patio. His apartment was a decent size in square footage, clean, cozy, warm, and inviting. He had plenty of windows which brightened up his place. He had a wonderful home. I was impressed. It looked better than my apartment building. He proudly showed me furniture pieces that Mrs. Irene had given him to help furnish his place along with some other pieces that his family brought for him. He had a fully furnished apartment that exceeding our expectations.

I had to be in his apartment maybe an hour when his cell phone rang and it was another woman calling him. I could tell that it was a woman when his demeanor changed. He went into another room to talk to her but when he returned to where I was sitting he received an ear full of complaining from me. He tried to justify his actions by telling me that I never told him how I felt about him. I was ready to head back home. Carlos walked me back to the train station in the dark and left me there to wait for the train by myself. I looked back to watch Carlos walk away wondering why I let my feelings get hurt by Carlos. I was letting my walls down for a player and a man who couldn't even make sure that I was safe. When the train arrived I told the conductor that I didn't have the money to ride but that I was trying to get back home. The conductor allowed me to ride for free.

Laying on my bed wondering what man God had for me was making me go crazy. Not only was I let down with Carlos to include that I was frustrated that I allowed myself to think that another man who I knew when I was a teenager was the man that God had for me. I found myself fantasizing that this man was my Boaz as if he was going to save me. I knew in my heart that Carlos could not possibly be the one for me. Although I was willing to compromise with knowing about his two different baby mama's, that he smoked cigarettes and cursed. I knew deep down that I couldn't compromise my beliefs and the way that Carlos treated me at his apartment only confirmed what I already knew.

In my mind, the only other option of who God truly had for me was this young fellow who I grew up with as a child in Alabama. Many moons ago I had a crush on this young fellow. When we were teens we shared a kiss at his auntie's house. When this young fellow went off to college that's when the sparks started to fly for me because he called. I never saw him as a boyfriend type but once he called it all changed for me. He was constantly on my mind. We talked every day for weeks. He even asked to come to visit me in Illinois which I looked forward to. I began to think about that kiss and with his phone calls just made me think about a future with this young fellow. I kept these feelings to myself as I didn't know what to do with them. He lived far away from me but I anticipated his arrival so that we could reconnect.

We talked for several weeks then suddenly the telephone calls stopped. He wasn't available when I called him and he didn't return my phone calls. My hopes were crushed when this young fellow began to be too busy to talk to me. I thought it was best that I disconnect from him by scratching out his phone number out of my phone book. If I didn't have a way to call him then my desire to want to talk to him would disappear.

I moved on with my life and married my boyfriend and shortly moved to New Jersey. Only a few months of living in New Jersey that's when I learned that this young fellow had been drafted in the NFL to a team in New Jersey. I was a married woman so my only thoughts were to try to connect with this young fellow from my hometown. I was excited about his new life and I wanted to be included in some part even if it was to be supportive. I made several attempts to talk to him by leaving a voice message on his cell phone and sending him messages through his personal email. He never returned my messages which seemed kind of odd to me. But I knew that he was busy and I needed to be more focused on my suffering marriage.

When I moved out of the shelter into my studio apartment I learned that the young fellow had moved into the same neighborhood right after me. Now if this was not the Lord who made it clear to me that this man belonged in my life then I didn't know what other signs a sista needed. It didn't bother me that he had a girlfriend. He always had a girlfriend. I put a rush on this mission to help the Lord out. Christmas was coming and his grandmother told me that she was coming to New Jersey to spend the holiday with this young fellow and his girlfriend. In my heart, I believed that once we saw each other then he would gravitate to me. It's all very simple. I was extremely fascinated with his new lifestyle and I wanted to be a part of it in some way. I fantasized about what outfit I would wear and what I would do with my hair. When Christmas came around I couldn't get a hold of his grandmother. He had her busy so I didn't get to meet her even though she was down the street from me. Not only was my feelings hurt but I was a little upset. The more that he rejected me the more I wanted to talk and see him. I found out where this young fellow townhouse was located. I asked Pretty Eyes to walk with me to bypass his townhouse. I already told Pretty Eyes and all of my friends even my mother that this man was my future husband. I felt strongly about this although this young fellow was not giving me any reason to believe that he was indeed my future mate. Something was telling me inside that he was my husband but I couldn't tell if it was God. I was starting to confuse myself. Being a Christian I know that not everybody sees God's plan for their life.

As Pretty Eyes and I were walking past this man's townhouse I looked to see which one was his place. I found out exactly where he lived by watching him tell it on a show where celebrities showed off their homes. I didn't feel like I was a stalker. I didn't show up at any of his games nor did I find out where he was dining or anything like that.

I sent him messages through his social media and once I believed that he directed a question to his followers asking them if they too had a stalker? I told my mother and she told me to stop trying to reach out to him. I didn't understand him as he didn't reply to any of my many attempts. My mother said some people forget where they came from and they forget the people too. I took my mother's advice and decided to quit trying to reach out to him. I should have probably taken the hint before. I was convinced that he was a part of my future but now I was confused and emotional. I began to pick up a weird habit that I use to do when I was a kid now

I was an adult because I wasn't settled and I wasn't stable in my mind.

I went to church after all of the confusion to hear the word of God. I was sitting in my usual place when I looked up and noticed a gentleman who didn't look like he belonged. When he opened the door to the sanctuary, there was a bright light hovering over him. He looked like he was from a foreign country. He was tall with hips that were kind of wide. His face, color of his skin, and his hair showed me that he was from another country, I assumed. I was very protective of my church. I had seen enough crazy news of people entering churches to attack, and that was not about to go down on my watch. The church service was coming to an end, so I leaped up and walked towards the door where this strange man entered. He had sat down. I walked out of the service to walk back in and I sat down next to him to make sure nothing would go down. As soon as I sat down, he placed his soft hands on my arm and leaned in my ear to whisper that God had a man for me, that he was working on him for me. Then this man quoted two scriptures to me. I was so stunned that he knew what to say to me that I stood back up and walked back to my seat. After the service, as I was leaving the sanctuary, I noticed that this same man was standing against the wall and I walked past him. I never said a thing to him and I forgot the scriptures he gave me, but I never forgot what he said, which gave me comfort and peace of mind not to worry about who my mate was. God had that under control.

Pretty Eyes came with me a couple of times to visit my church. She didn't sit with me and Isabella as she wanted to sit on a different side. However, we came together. Isabella and I would always have such a good time praising God in dance, holding hands to pray. Pretty Eyes and I sat in her mother's van in the parking lot before the service. She confided in me that she found out that her boyfriend was married. She said that she never knew that he was married after all of the years they had been together. Now she was hurt in the reason that he had a family and now she was pregnant with his baby. I had nothing to say, but I sure was thinking that he told her that I was using her. He made it like I was shady when he was the shady one. I felt bad for Pretty Eyes, but I knew that God would have an answer for her. She went on to say that her boyfriend had plans to end his marriage and that he was separated. Well, we went into the church service and I sat in my usual spot next to Isabella and Pretty Eyes sat in another spot. God heard everything we discussed in that girl's car because he used my pastor to deliver a message. The pastor said the man that you are waiting for is not going to leave his wife. Oh, man, the pastor had so much to say pertaining to our discussion on that pulpit. I just knew that Pretty Eyes knew that this message was directed to her. The only thing the pastor didn't do was call her by name. I left the church service, excited to follow up with Pretty Eyes to comfort her and to warn her. She kept quiet, but I let her know that the message was for her.

When I arrived home my neighbor Kim and I walked to our local Rite Aid for some medicine. Kim said that she had a headache, so I went with her. When we got to Rite Aid, I went straight to the medicine aisle while she went to a different aisle and then she came and stood next to me, asking me to look for a certain brand that I never heard of before. She stood close beside me, looking as well, but we couldn't find what she was seeking. As we were headed out of the store, one of the managers approached us, immediately accusing us of stealing medicine from the aisle we were standing in. He asked us to show him our purses. I didn't have a problem with that because I knew that I didn't steal anything nor did I see Kim steal anything. This incident reminded me of a time when I was a teenager and was falsely accused of stealing clothes in front of people. So I had no problem showing this security officer my purse, as I did when I was a young lady. I had nothing to hide because I was not a thief. I didn't care to show him my bag, however, Kim had a major problem with it and she made it known that she was not going to show him her bag and she recited her rights to the manager. Well, this manager kept accusing and arguing with Kim. She wouldn't even listen to me when I asked her to open her purse to show him. The manager threatened to call the police on us, and Kim urged him to do so. But then the manager kicked us out of the store and ordered us to stay away. We were not allowed to step foot back into his store. He said that he had us on camera stealing, but that was not true since I knew that I didn't steal a thing and Kim was adamant that she didn't. I don't know what that was all about, but I was upset and so was Kim. She told her fiancé about it and she talked about this incident for days afterward.

I went to the daycare center to vent to the teacher whose church I went to visit for the baptism about what happened at Rite Aid. She calmed me down by encouraging me to continue to shop in that store. I did nothing wrong, so there was no reason for this manager to ban me. I continued to shop, but I felt the eyes of the workers watching me. Whenever I went to the store I didn't go with Kim, so it wouldn't be obvious who we were and to keep it all peaceful for my sake.

I walked around the town with Pretty Eyes, as she had gotten bigger with her pregnancy and looked really good. The only thing that gained weight was her belly. Everything else about her remained small. She was the most beautiful pregnant lady I ever laid eyes on. Since being pregnant, Pretty Eyes seemed to be enjoying her pregnancy. She moved into her mother's attic. Her boyfriend kept feeding her the line that he was going to leave his wife and they would be a family. In Pretty Eyes mind he gave her no reason for doubt, other than he had kept his marriage a secret. He tried to make it all better by showering Pretty Eyes with whatever she needed. He spoiled her by giving her money, buying her a new white down comforter, and one of those fans that needed a remote control and supposedly blew out cool air and heat. I made frequent visits to her to talk about life and keep her company. She was just as driven as she was when she was not pregnant still attending networking events and walking around town.

As far as my job search went I remained vigilant. I wasn't going to settle, but time was winding down for my housing assistance to be done. It was almost a full year that I was accepting government assistance and once that year was over and done then it was my responsibility to pay my rent. I had a job interview as a leasing consultant that Chris had taken me while he had a vacation from his job. Sadly I wasn't offered the job however I remained hopeful that I was getting close to a job offer. I constantly made time for my friends as they did for me too. Pretty Eyes' life was evolving. Isabella was working in the medical field, earning really good money. She surprised me and gave me $150. She said that she had extra money left after she paid her bills and asked God what to do with that extra money. She told me that God told her to give the money to me. I was elated and appreciative. I later found out while visiting her that Isabella was married when her stepfather blurted the news. I was taken aback, as I thought that she was too young to be married and I had no idea, as she did not share this piece of information with me. I confronted her with this new news, as I realized that she did have two different last names that she went by. Her response was that she did tell me, but I knew for a fact that she didn't.

I would not have forgotten something that important. And to make matters interesting, she was married to the new maintenance man of my apartment building. Isabella told me that his mother and her mother were friends coming out of Columbia together. The parents arranged this illegal marriage to keep Isabella in the states. At that point, I figured this was none of my business. She wasn't even the person who initially told me. I just let Isabella live her life and hoped that she wasn't keeping any more secrets. She claimed that she didn't like him beyond being friends. I had a hard time believing that since he was not bad looking. I stayed overnight at her house when the maintenance man came knocking on their door, seemingly intoxicated and needed a place to lay his head. Isabella opened the door for him and we got him situated in their basement. The dynamics of their relationship were strange. You could tell that they were just friends but they did have a deeper relationship even though they never let on that they were married. He received his mail at their house and how comfortable he was to come over her house in the middle of the night was interesting.

As we were talking, we heard this hard bang coming from upstairs. We slowly crept up the stairs to see what that commotion was all about. Isabella's parents' front door was violently kicked in. Isabella's brother kicked the door down, wearing an all-black outfit. He was out of the house when no one knew. Instead of knocking on the door, he kicked their front door in, causing damage. He woke up everyone in the house, including her parents. He was erratic and difficult to settle. Her family didn't seem as sweet as I thought, and Isabella was hiding stuff from me, which I wished she hadn't. However, I kept coming to her house now even more, since I knew her younger brother had anger issues. I grew close to her family and wanted to make sure they were all right. I spent the night frequently at her house, watching movies and eating home-cooked meals, which her mother cooked every night. When we watched movies, her brother would secretly hack a system to get us to watch new releases for free. At first, I felt weird being this Christian girl watching movies like this, but I just kept my thoughts and opinions to myself, relaxed and savored the moments with Isabella.

Her brother is extremely smart and handsome. Although he spent most of his days shut up in his bedroom doing God knows what. He was book smart and clever but lazy and had a foul mouth. One day at the house he blurted out an insulting word that as a black woman was offensive. I was, even more, shocked that he said it around Isabella with me there, and she had no response other than a little smirk. I also learned about Isabella's frequent cussing. If you didn't know Isabella and only seen her once, you would think that she was this sweet soft spoken girl who goes to church regularly jumping out windows to attend bible study. You wouldn't

believe that she was secretly married, cusses, and embel-
lishes on the stories that she tells.

God has blessed me with an abundance of friendships.
We all had areas in which God was working on us. Every
turn God had someone taking care of me although we had
colorful backgrounds. Every so often Christina insisted that I
go shopping with her to Kohl's clothing store. I grew to learn
that Christina had a system. She would print a couple of coupons on top of coupons. By the time we walked out of Kohl's,
she had a bag filled with free clothes. She always shared by
handing me a shirt or two. I saw this as an opportunity to talk
to her about Jesus, planting seeds in her mind, in a loving
way, that going to a guru was not the place for her and that
she should try going back to church. She was all about peace
and love and she didn't think that the church could give her
that. She was still wounded over the people that gossiped
and caused strife in the church house. I could respect and
understand her point. The only thing that I could do was to be
that role model, to show her that not all Christians behaved
that way. It was my mission to be a light to prove that not all
Christians were hypocrites. They meant what they said by
living it day by day.

I had Isabella and Christina to talk to about celibacy. It felt
good to have these ladies walking the same path as I was
when it came to waiting on God to bring our men into our
lives and wait until marriage for lovemaking. But along our
journey, Christina met a mechanic who befriended her. She
had been celibate for seven years, now this mechanic was
in her ear, telling her sweet nothings, and she fell for his trap.
Although she knew that this man had a live-in girlfriend, he
also told her a story that she believed and she slept with him
in his dirty garage where he had all of his filthy mechanic's
stuff. Afterward, she regretted it but she fell right back into
his mind control and gave up her body yet again to this man
in his mechanic's shop. Finally, after the girlfriend rolled up
on them and he got caught, he got Christina, the peace and
love girl, stirred up in some mess and now it became violent.

She got some common sense but it took a while for her to leave this mechanic man alone. She would purposely drive past his shop and sometimes ask where he was, but it seemed that he was ducking and diving her. I sat in her car observing this and thinking, "poor lady," but I never said a word. She would have to learn this hard lesson on her own. Yet I still tried to be a friend to her, even going to dinner with her and her daughter at my favorite restaurant, Fridays.

We sat in the restaurant and I ordered my favorite meal that I always ordered. I am a woman of habit. I wondered why the waiters didn't clear our table as we finished eating our meals. I finally stood up when I saw a pile of old plates and food still on our table. I pulled the waiter to the side to voice my concern in private when he told me that it was not anything personal to me but that the two women I was sitting with came in about a week ago and caused a major scene with the team. They kept sending orders back and were rude customers. He asked me to please not be mad, but this had nothing to do with me. I stood there baffled, but I had to walk away knowing that I wasn't able to join Christina and her daughter at that restaurant ever again. I graciously went back to our table not mentioning a word. Christina was driving me to my apartment, getting on the highway then suddenly the car behind us slightly bumped the back of her car. She pulled over to the side as did the other car. They exchanged information and a few days later Christina saw me at Workforce asking me if my neck was hurting. It seemed a bit deceitful because she kept asking me the same question after I told her that I was not hurt. And to be honest I didn't think that she was either but she seemed to be convincing to his insurance and received a settlement. She tried to convince me to see a doctor after I refused because I too could get a settlement but I learned my lesson about lying in desperate times.

A couple of days after she received her settlement check I rode with her when she dropped her daughter off at college, I made an attempt to talk to Christina about God and turning her life over to Jesus, but she wasn't hearing me, so I made a judgment call to no longer stay friends with her. I felt in my heart that I was her friend long enough and usually I was not close friends with people who did not share the same faith. I felt like my time with her had expired. From that time I made no attempts to reach out to her. We fell out of contact.

Pretty Eyes due date to deliver her baby was definitely here. I received a phone call while at the kid's center from her sister to please come to the hospital. I didn't have a way, so I politely asked one of the office workers if they could drop me off. When I arrived at the hospital I was told that Pretty Eyes had a miscarriage. She carried her baby all the way to delivery, but the baby died. This was devastating news. The other sad part was that the baby daddy was nowhere to be found. He didn't visit her at the hospital, giving her some lame excuses. I stayed with her the entire time, even lying next to her, waiting for her baby daddy to come and pick us up, but he never showed up. As a matter of fact, he had his cousin to show up and pick both of us up at the hospital hours later. This was pathetic that a man would do this to the woman that he claimed to love. Not only that, but they both just lost their child and he was nowhere around.

Pretty Eyes did not deserve that. Pretty Eyes had a difficult time, but she did her best to stay strong. Her baby's father did show up for the funeral and I sang at the burial, "His eyes are on the sparrow." Still, her boyfriend became distant and dismissed her. He wasn't around like he used to be, and guess what: he never left his wife. He kept getting caught in lie after lie. I continued to be supportive of Pretty Eyes by going to visit her and keeping my mouth shut. I wouldn't know what to say if I did speak other than I was sorry for her loss and showing her that.

Faith in God

Those around me were concerned about what I was going to do since my government assistance was about to end. It was coming close to being a full year of receiving housing and I had no job offers, nor any interviews lined up, however, I stayed in faith. I kept answering people the same as I did in the beginning, that God would bless me with a perfect job at the perfect time. God's will would be done for my life, not my will and not anyone else's will for my life. Kim asked me while we stood outside in the cool breeze what I was going to do. She suggested that I try to live in those hotels where they put you in, and I remembered the man, Tom, who lived in the roach- and a bedbug-infested hotel where they put him in. I refused that suggestion while Kim seemed to be concerned for me. I let Kim know with confidence that I was waiting on Jesus and that He would come through as He's kept me all this time. He hasn't failed me. God would come through.

I sent my resume to a hotel that I found on Craigslist for their Night Audit position that they had posted. They scheduled an interview with me and I kept my composure. It seemed incredibly perfect for me the moment that I laid my eyes on this job. In my heart, I knew that I had the position before the interview. I took the bus to this interview not knowing where to get off. I was extremely happy to have finally landed an interview with a job that wasn't far from where I lived. It wasn't walking distance but I could take one local bus straight to the job. I even mentioned to the bus driver that I was on my way to a job interview. Instead of dropping me off at the back of the mall that's across the street from the hotel. The bus driver dropped me off right in front of the hotel, which was not his route.

I felt the interview went well. I answered all of the questions with a smile. In that interview, the assistant general manager asked me about my volunteer work and she was impressed that I had such a resume that included volunteering with children, which meant that I was caring, and she was equally impressed with my education at the Bible College. She wanted me to expound on those two alone. I had many jobs on my resume, but these two she wanted to know about.

I returned to the Workforce where one of the instructors grew concerned for my well-being. This new instructor grew to care for me a great deal. Once she was homeless and lived in the same shelter that I lived in. She could relate which made her that much more interested in helping me as much as possible. She now worked for Workforce as one of their instructors and was engaged to be married with three little children. I would sit in her class and just admire her strength and courage to speak in front of students every week. She admired how I listened and followed instructions. She saw that I was trying to do my best. I would come to visit her on her breaks and we'd engage in conversations about life in general. We were friendly with each other. She hit the panic button and ran up the stairs of her office building to see about getting me an extension for my housing assistance. From my understanding, this is not allowed to receive government assistance for housing once you have reached your limit but this instructor was about to be an advocate for me. She wanted me to volunteer as a worker under her this way I could help her run her classroom and in return, I could possibly get that housing extension.

While I sat downstairs getting ready for a meeting with Steve to see about extending me, I received a phone call from the hotel, offering me the job. God had the lady to run up the elevator to deliver the news to me. I was tearfully happy that God came through for me and proved Himself not only to me but to those people that were around me. My faith in God would not waver and here He came through in the nick of time. I started the new position within a week.

I interviewed for the overnight position, however, the leaders at this hotel thought it best that I worked the front desk during the day. They thought that I should have more interaction with the guest since I had a wonderful smile and a bubbly personality. They agreed to allow me to work the second shift of 3 pm until 11 pm. I started work the exact day that my rental assistance stopped. God is amazing to give me a job after not working for over a year. He sent me this job just at the perfect time just like what I was telling people. Now that I was starting my new job I would have to be behind rent for a month. I told the landlord about my situation and he seemed to be empathetic and understanding where he didn't pressure me to catch up. This job was a miracle. It's everything that I asked God for. It was decent in pay where I had enough money to pay my bills and still have fun. Granted I didn't have enough money to catch up on the one month of rent but I was hopeful that I would be able to pay my rent moving forward. I went online to find out how to commute back and forth to work. Before my shift starts, I would take a bus where the bus stop is close to my apartment building, take that bus straight to the mall, and then I would walk across the street to my hotel. After work around 11:20 pm I would take a bus where the bus is in front but to the side of the hotel building. That bus would drop me off at the train station near my job and then I would ride the train to my town and walk home around 11:50 pm. I really appreciate the time that I had taken the train to and from Carlos apartment. I felt comfortable taking public transportation on a regular basis without fear. Immediately I called Isabella, Pretty Eyes, and Chris about my job. They were ecstatic for the door that God had opened for me. We planned to celebrate but first I had to get settled.

My first week of work I had to attend orientation. The bus driver dropped me off in front of the mall so that I could run across the street instead of dropping me off behind the mall like he was supposed to. In the week of orientation, we ended the sessions early. As I was walking out of the front doors of this hotel to walk across the street, I was stopped by Tiffany. I turned around and gazed at her for a minute, we then hugged each other. Tiffany just started working at the same hotel as the overnight supervisor. How weird it was that New Jersey was enormous, the person who I used to live with was standing right in front of me, working at the same place at the same time as me. She was also a new hire. She just finished her new hire orientation a week before I started. We talked briefly before I quickly walked across the street to catch my bus to go home.

The next couple of days was odd. Tiffany and I hadn't talked nor seen each other ever since I left her house almost a year ago, yet here we were working for the same company. I felt in my heart that God had orchestrated this for a reason. I didn't know why but it had to serve a greater purpose for God to reconnect us like this. The odd part was that I found myself consoling Tiffany at the workplace each time she worked her overnight shift. When Tiffany came into work to relieve me I found myself staying to listen to her complain about how her bosses were treating her even wiping the tears from her face. Tiffany was miserable and often times she complained while her bosses were standing close to me.

The bus that I had to catch to go home was not always reliable. A few nights, Isabella and her brother came to pick me up when the bus didn't. I had to call the transportation service to file a complaint because the bus failed to pick a few of us up while we stood outside in the night waiting. Eventually, some people walked home while others like myself had to call a cab or call someone they knew. Thank God that Isabella's mom allowed her to pick me up in their family SUV. Isabella and her mom cooked me dinner and were elated that I was able to find a job. I profusely praised Jesus, that it was all God who did the blessing. I wanted to share this good news with Kim, but she moved out of the apartment with her fiancé into a house they were renting. Boy, this girl was moving on up in life and I was profoundly proud of their accomplishments. But then I ran into her fiancé while I was walking the streets. He was attending the AA meetings. He shared with me that Kim went to drug court and they did a drug test, which she failed, and she got sent to jail. It hurt my heart to hear in that I witnessed her strive to be the best she could. I felt bad that she fell back into that lifestyle of drugs when she was doing so well. She had a different job that paid better than the one she had, she had a pet cat, she was engaged, and she moved into a house. For her to be sent back to jail was terrible and a major setback. With her failing her drug test made me wonder about the situation at Rite Aid. Did she, in fact, take the medicine and boldly lie to me in my face and that manager. She was adamant about not allowing him to look into her bags. I can't believe that she would put me in that kind of predicament. I really hope that Kim is able to change and bounce back once she's given another chance. I continued to lift Kim up in prayer. It was about dang time that I got my life together. God blessed me with two poetry books, I was still able to keep my website and now I was working a full-time job. Blessings to the God of miracles.

I stood at the bus waiting on the bus so that I can get to work on time. During my wait, two men pulled up in a truck and stopped in front of me at the red traffic light. The passenger guy kept trying to get my attention but I ignored him. He then yelled out, "That's why you at the bus stop waiting on the bus." I thought to myself, how rude! I just rolled my eyes, looked the other way, and kept quiet. This bus situation was complicating. If I didn't have some random man yelling at me. I also had to be disappointed by the bus not picking me up after work. The first couple of weeks of the bus deciding to skip our route I could call Isabella and she would swiftly pick me up. She then stopped picking up her cell phone whenever I called. She later told me that her mother stopped handing her the truck keys and wouldn't allow her to come. I walked back inside the hotel trying to figure out how in the world I was getting back to my apartment. But before I could be overly concerned the front desk manager offered to drive me to my apartment whenever we worked together which was every night. She said that it was on her way to her house. I gladly accepted and thanked God all the way home. She took me for several months until she got fired yet her replacement the manager Kory lived in my town and worked my shift. He said that he would take me home and drop me off at the nearby shopping center. As I walked home in the night I would see police cars parked in various places. Whenever I passed them by I would thank God for their presence. I walked home with a sense of peace, gratification, and security knowing that I was in my Father's hand. I also thanked God for placing me in the hearts of man to shower me with so much favor and blessings.

How gratifying it is for me to have a job. I was out of work for two years, searching for work nonstop, enduring all of the pain and hardships, and God came and saved the day. He made the promise that He would never leave me nor forsake me. He said that He would provide perfect provisions and He has not let me down. Even with all the struggles, there's still manna sent down from heaven. God's hand is never short. Although I didn't cook food at home my job prepared dinner for the staff every night. I never went without. These types of blessings remind me of a scripture that my mom likes to quote, Psalm 37:25, "I have been young, and now am old; yet have I not seen the righteous forsaken, nor his seed begging bread."

I arrived at the mall that's across the street from my job like two hours before my shift started. Usually, I sat down on a chair and watched people walk by. Now, this mall was exquisite, celebrity stars shopped here such as the likes of Wendy Williams, pro athletes, to name a few. This mall had stores that I couldn't pronounce. This place was by far one of the most beautiful shopping malls I ever laid eyes on. Once I was on the escalator with my big hair when a woman approached me and asked if she just saw me on TV.

I brought my Joel Osteen book to read at the mall before my shift started since I was there for a long period of time. I'm reading my book when this cute Korean-looking young lady, who seemed to be a college student, approached me to ask if I could take a sweater back to a store where her brother had purchased it within the mall. She needed my help in returning it since her brother had lost the receipt and tag. Now, this question seemed strange and odd to me. I didn't quite understand what she was asking, so I politely told her that I wasn't able to do that. She walked away and tried to ask me the same thing again, and I politely told her no. The third time she came I just looked at her as she told me that her brother was going off to college and they really needed help. She looked like a nice young lady who wasn't going to take no for an answer. I thought that I could help her out before I headed to work. I put my Joel Osteen book down and took her bag and proceeded to go upstairs to the store this young lady led me to. She told me that she would be downstairs and wait for me by the elevator after I got the money back from the store. To no surprise that store had strict rules that if you didn't have the tag or receipt you could not return the item. I didn't put up a fight. I understood. Besides I didn't want to be in there in the first place.

On my way out of the store to deliver the bad news to this young lady. I looked down to see this same young lady talking to a tall big black man. They didn't even look like they should know each other, yet she was talking to him comfortably. When I watched these two without them knowing that I was looking at them. They seemed to be discussing the plan what seemed like on the sneak tip by their body language. Instantly I knew in my heart that I was con into this. I came down with a fire inside of me that this girl tricked me, interrupted my peace and I fell for it but she wasn't standing at the elevator when I approached the big tall black man. I pressed the bag into his chest as I told him to deliver this message to his friend that the store wouldn't receive the item. I turned and walked away, turning the corner to head out of the mall to walk across the street to my job in anger of what just happened.

Here I was this innocent soul minding my own business to be interrupted by Satan and his little helpers while I am sitting down reading a Joel Osteen book. I was definitely not ready for that kind of crime that just crept up on me. I could have gotten into trouble for something that I had no idea about. How could I fall so quickly for this? Trying to return a stolen item. I should have known better but I had a different idea of what criminals looked like, where they hung out, and how they handled their crimes. I learned by this incident that not all crimes happen in the hood and not all criminals look like they were thuggish out and they weren't all men. Some were cute little women that looked like a suburban college student.

I called Chris because he always seemed to calm me down. He always had a good listening ear. Then I called Isabella. Isabella told me that she had a vision at the same time that I had the incident with the young lady and man. She said that someone was trying to come after me, but there was a glass that prevented them from coming to follow me. I said that it was that guy trying to follow me, but God wouldn't let him. Isabella said that this glass was like a wall so he couldn't come chase after me. The angels and this glass wall wouldn't let him. She told me that she was praying for me at this exact moment. Man, I really appreciated her prayers because the Lord knew that I needed it.

Tiffany quit the hotel job. We hugged and said our good-byes. I wondered why did God have us to reconnect like this? Maybe God was showing her that I was doing alright and for us to make amends. I hope this is the case because I'm grateful to her for opening her home to me just when I was about to get kicked out of Santrese townhouse. God used her to be a blessing to me and I am eternally thankful. In return, I pray that I sowed some seeds in her life.

The first month of working at the hotel, we had a grand opening of the spa. It was a huge success. The hotel transformed the lobby to being all white. We had famous celebrities and models coming through. I even saw Tyson the model walking by. He didn't look my way but kept looking straight as he walked. He was handsome and a lot shorter than I could have imagined. The famous singer Seal was the live entertainment in our ballroom. The workers, including myself, snuck downstairs to hear his wonderful voice sing and to see him in action. Seal has a unique, powerful, beautiful, and captivating voice. Now I see why people around the world love to hear him sing. His vocals are out of this world. That night I became a fan.

Then my job offered free massages to the employees so that when guests inquired about their services, we could give an answer. I was super excited because boy, did I need it and it couldn't have come at a better time. I had this older woman with the hands that seemed to have massaged my knots in my back and shoulders away. This lady had hands that could send you straight to heaven. How did I get blessed so fast like this? Only by the hands of God to have me feel special as I transitioned to the next chapter of my life. I walked in the room to prepare for my massage in a white robe, lay down among candles and soothing music. I could have stayed in that room all day long. Just what the good Lord ordered. I didn't have any money to tip this lady. I really wanted to tip her for doing such a fantastic job. She seemed to be understanding as I walked away apologizing but feeling like I experienced heaven down here on earth. My God was in the blessing business, Deuteronomy 31:6, "Be strong and of a good courage, fear not, nor be afraid of them: for the LORD thy God, he it is that doth go with thee; he will not fail thee, nor forsake thee."

My job catered to celebrities, influential people, along with customers who made the kind of money that you only dreamed about. Women and men who dressed with eloquence and sophistication. I couldn't help myself, but compliment most of the customers. I never worked in a place with this much esteem before. I complimented this one lady from head to toe. I started by complimenting her hair then her outfit and shoes but when I got to her jewelry. She stopped me in my tracks by asking me, if I was checking her out. I could tell by her reaction that I made her be on the offense which made me feel uncomfortable. I learned to scale it back a little. My co-workers didn't see it as a big deal to have all this substance in the midst of us however I see it differently. In the word of God, it says, Proverbs 22:29, "Seest thou a man diligent in his business? He shall stand before kings; he shall not stand before mean men."

I had to work on adjusting the way of thinking. I went from being restricted and having no voice so that I wouldn't be sanctioned. Now God placed me at a job that demanded that I use my voice, that what I had to say mattered. My bosses urged me to be more confident while assisting the customers. They kept trying to help me see that I had the authority to make decisions. I was working on becoming a better version of myself. My plan in life was to walk in wisdom, knowledge, and understanding. To discern when to speak, when not to speak, when to embrace when not to embrace. I needed to be wiser so that I didn't lose my job as I have in the past. I longed to make moves differently.

I published my second book, LIFE. I got the rights back to my book and then I got a new job. This was a great feeling. Now I was ready to start the process of introducing my two books to the world. I was on a roll. Nothing could hold me back from victory. I had a lot to celebrate. Thanksgiving rolled around and Isabella and I spent that holiday with Chris for the second time. We all had a lot to celebrate. I spent Christmas with Isabella's family, and around the Christmas tree, we all gave each other presents. Pretty Eyes reached out to me and told me to come to her house, she had something to give to me. When I got to her place, she was sitting in the kitchen. She handed me her red Louis Vuitton bag that was wrapped, the bag that she carried around with her everywhere. She also gave me some jewelry and other precious items that once was dear to her. She told me that she wanted to get rid of everything that her ex-boyfriend gave to her. She wanted to start off fresh and didn't want to keep anything from his cheating behind. She asked God who to give her most valuable possessions to, and she said that God told her to give them to me. I was stunned yet appreciative in my mind when

I walked back to my apartment. I was thinking this was the same man who told Pretty Eyes that I was using her and now I was being gifted with the items he gave to her, Proverbs 13:22, "A good man leaveth an inheritance to his children's children: and the wealth of the sinner is laid up for the just."

All these gifts that Pretty Eyes had given me, I tucked away at the top of my closet, hoping that I would wear those nice gifts one day for the TV interviews for my books. Also, Mrs. Irene had given me a bag of clothes from her grandkids and their parents. Mrs. Irene was beginning to give me a bag of clothes for every new season we were entering. I appreciated every outfit. I shared the clothes that looked youthful with Isabella. Most of the item of clothes Mrs. Irene gave to me was beyond precious. And when the holiday including my birthday came around she handed me a card with hundreds of dollars in it.

Winter time had come and it was getting extremely cold for me to be traveling by public transportation. I did what my mother told me to do which was to pray every day to God for my new car. The first two weeks while riding the bus I prayed to ask God for a car and then after the two weeks I stopped asking God for the car. I began to thank Him for my car.

This job came with many perks such as getting tipped 50 dollar bills from customers on a weekly, to free spa treatments, and free dinners every night that I worked. But my favorite perk was servicing the NFL, NBA, and hockey teams. Oh my goodness these men were tall and handsome. I couldn't even control myself. When I was younger hanging out in the night clubs I use to wonder where the athletes hang out. I would inquire but my hang out buddies could care less. All they wanted to do was dance the night away with a gentleman while my appetite was strangely different. I could never find these athletes no matter how hard I tried. How funny that once I gave my life to the Lord that the men I searched for appeared at my place of employment. I no longer had to seek them. I was extra by applying my makeup heavy on my face and wearing costume jewelry galore. I would talk loudly and butt in conversations. These athletes paid me no mind.

Whenever I came to work I still desired to work the overnight shift. I watched about five people get hired for the position and leave quickly. Some people would get trained for one day and never returned the following night for their shift. They complained about the nasty attitudes of the overnight staff. One of the gentlemen felt that the work was overloaded. Usually, the overnight shift was more laid back, do as you please, but not this job. The night shift had work to do from sundown to sunset. It was demanding and the overnight team was intense. However, this didn't deter me from desiring to work the overnight shift. I wanted the extra pay and I felt that by me working the overnight shift that I could work on my other projects during the day.

When I applied for the position, they were so desperate that they hired me when I inquired. Usually, we were supposed to stay within the company holding the same position for a year before we could transfer to a different position. I applied at the perfect time where they couldn't afford to turn me away. It was a win-win situation. I would start my new position immediately.

Mrs. Irene called me to let me know that one of her friend's father wanted to give away his car. It was a Buick in good condition, an older car that he rarely drove. However, he couldn't drive it anymore and wanted to give the car away at no charge. Irene thought about me and told her friend to give the car to me. I met her friend at the library and gave her a dollar to get the car keys. I took a cab to the DMV to switch the tag and get a new license plate. I then took the cab to her friend's father's house to get the car, and I drove off in the Buick to my home. I had taken my mother's advice about praying for a car. Now here my prayers were answered. God moved in the heart of man to give me a car without paying for it. It was an older car but in great condition. The inside and out of the car was clean and well maintained. The car drove smoothly.

I had to go and swoop my buddy Isabella up from her house to take her on a joy ride. We didn't get out of her block when my car stopped without notification on the road. We were still in front of her house. Then her landlord who happens to be her neighbor came outside to try to figure out what was the problem. He told me that my car needed anti-freeze, but in the meantime, he would replace that with water and that should work for a week. But my car was not having that. The car stopped again, and I knew that I had to take my new baby to the shop. I named my Buick Horsey because she was big and powerful. I took Horsey to the gas station where they did mechanical work too. While they were placing antifreeze in my car, they also told me that I needed two axles replaced. The total cost would be $800. That sounded a bit steep and definitely out of my budget. I heard of a car mechanic closer to my apartment building who was more reasonable in price, but when I drove my car to this shop, the owner of the establishment was awfully rude to me and acted like he didn't need my money, so I left.

I was driving my car to get a new wig on the main road when suddenly a ball rolled out on the street, which I ran over. A black little boy came out of nowhere to pick it up. I didn't see his face, only that he was a boy, which was weird to me because I'd never seen children playing in that area before. There were houses along the road, but not where a kid would dare to play. That was odd, but I kept driving. I made it to the shop but surely on my way home I had a flat tire. Isabella and her stepfather told me to go to the shop on the corner. The same shop where the owner had been rude to me. I told them what happened, so they escorted me back to his shop and spoke to him in Spanish. His attitude towards me took a 360.

That owner of the shop Jose did a good job. I continued to go to him after this since he seemed to care for my business. I had to take care of some small things that rusted from the years of this car parked in the garage. Other than that, the car ran smoothly and I kept it clean. I took Horsey to get vac-uumed and washed every two weeks. I was proud that God blessed me. I had a car, an apartment, a job, food in my belly, health, great friendships that surrounded me, and my family and I were starting to speak again. My world was blessed.

I went back to the daycare center to visit with the teachers and let them see how I was doing. I knew that they cared. I also wanted to visit the children who didn't remember me. Even some of my favorite students didn't recognize me. This made me sad but the teachers let me know that this happens to them too. The kids forget you but I would never forget them. I will hold them in my memories forever and be forever grateful to the teachers at the daycare center. But once I walked out of the building I knew in my heart that I would not return. It was time that I moved on with my life. Use my past as lessons learned.

Iron sharpening Iron

At church, I let my hair down during praise and worship music and was among the saints. Pretty Eyes was starting to attend my church every Sunday. She was no longer attending her church. She even went through the member's classes and graduated. Now she was a member. She had a new look on life and desired to do things right this go around. She was dedicated to sanctifying herself. Our conversation shifted where we were sounding alike. 1 Corinthians 1:10, "Now I beseech you brethren, by the name of our Lord Jesus Christ, that ye all speak the same thing, and that there be no divisions among you; but that ye be perfectly joined together in the same mind and in the same judgment."

It was refreshing to finally have a conversation with her that didn't involve us disagreeing on the basics of the Christian walk. She wanted to go back to the shelter and start over. In my mind, when she presented this idea to me about what she was going to do, I agreed with her. I felt like she did it all wrong the first time but this go-round would benefit her. She moved back to the same shelter we left and they accepted her. But this didn't last long. When she got there, she had the mindset of starting over, and she stayed for about a month. She said that she needed her freedom and the month was just enough time for her to realize that she no longer needed to stay in a shelter. She moved in with different family members, even sleeping on the couch of one of her cousin, next to bulldogs they owned. I felt bad for her but she felt that she needed to go through these experiences in this season of her life.

All I wanted for her was for her to do well for herself. I wasn't sure where her life was going, but Pretty Eyes stayed in faith as I did. She always spoke positively. Never did she think that her moves were all wrong. As a matter of fact, she always said that God told her to do this or that. How could you argue with anyone or contest what they said when they said that God told them? She had her own relationship with God, so I trusted what she said. I mean, I had my own journey that seemed strange to people and I told them the same thing she was speaking, so I held my tongue and let her live her life.

Finally one of her aunties told her that she could come and stay with her in a calmer environment, where there weren't any dogs and she could sleep in her own room while she figured out what her next move was going to be. At first, her movements seemed very bright, until she met a handsome guy from her aunts' neighborhood. He told her sweet nothings in her ear and she fell into Satan's trap and slept with the man after she vowed to stay holy and not succumb to sexual behavior. She didn't even tell me at first. When she finally told me, she said that she felt like I would be disappointed in her. Like she let me down. Which she did. I listened to her and hoped that one day she would learn sooner than later. Well, she did learn when the man stopped returning her calls and when she popped over to his house, he started acting funny. That sexual relationship didn't last long. Pretty Eyes was ready to pack it up.

For the Fourth of July, I was off from work, which was rare in my business which is opened 24 hours 365 days a year. God told me to call my best friend, so I called Isabella, and she happened to be at home. I thought that she wouldn't be at home, yet there she was, saying that she was cleaning out her closet. I told her to get ready so that we could go out, my treat. I got dressed and we went to dinner at Applebee's, and I paid this time. Then her mother called to invite us to her job where they were hosting a Fourth of July party. When we got there at this mansion size of a house, we walked to the back of the house, where the yard went to a lake. I could see boats in the water, waiting for the Fourth of July action. This family also had a caterer, tables set up of finger food. Isabella and I walked to the backyard to sit down on a huge towel covering the grass to prepare ourselves for the fireworks. We were so close that the debris of the fireworks fell on top of our heads. It was surely a good time. Isabella and I talked about life and wanting that special somebody to be in our lives. We often had conversations like this, but she was way mature than I was when I was her age. I found myself encouraging her to not settle because God had the perfect man for her. She was so beautiful that men were trying so hard to come to her, but she had to be strong in the mind because the devil would try to trick her. I enjoyed talking and spending time with Isabella because I finally had a friend who related. It was iron sharpening iron. We were speaking the same language. We both wanted the same things in life. We wanted to wait for God to bless us with our husbands, we both were celibate, we both wanted to be in ministry.

Isabella had the softest hands. Once she showed me that her hands glittered sometimes, she believed that she had healing hands. We could tag team on people spiritually. I was looking forward to our growing friendship. Isabella has attended the same church, but she occasionally visited other people's churches. She had been in this movement where she visited different churches every week, and then she would pop into our church, sitting down like she'd been there every week. She told me that she had a dream that the world was going to end and so she went to visit churches delivering this message.

She started attending another church more frequently than her usual, where there was a young pastor. He took a liking to Isabella, especially when she announced that she was anointed by having healing hands. He then proceeded to tell her that God told him that she was his wife. I didn't know what happened, but it scared Isabella to come back to our church and she stayed for most Sundays, and when she was not at church she stayed home. Isabella told me that she was having suicidal thoughts. I knew that she was frustrated with her family hosting parties almost every weekend at their house. She didn't want to be in that torture of the mind in that secular world at her home, and her brother had frequent violent episodes. During the summer, her family went out of town, leaving him alone in the house. They asked me to go over to check on the house whenever I got the chance. I went over to their back door. He was in the living room, looking out the window, telling me that I was not needed. When I went to tell him that his parents wanted me to come by, he told me in a tone that made me believe him. I left and asked Pretty Eyes to ride with me to get the things that I left at Isabella's house.

It was hard for me to hear that Isabella was having suicidal thoughts. At church, she tried to tell our pastor after he finished preaching. But when she walked up to where Pastor was standing one of the ushers got in the way that prevented her from talking to the pastor.

CHAPTER SEVEN

God Never Fails

My work schedule didn't allow me to hang out with my friends. Isabella told me over the telephone that she was singing back up with Chris like how I use to. That news was kind of odd to me since Isabella never showed any interest in singing and she couldn't hold a note. However, I was supportive of her praising Jesus and getting her mind off of committing suicide. It was a good idea for her to spend quality time with other believers.

I had taken vacation days from work to spend Christmas with Isabella at Chris's house where he lived with the couple from church. This year we had plans to spend the night over his house for the weekend. Chris's house had a guest bedroom on the second floor across the hall from the married couple. This was a special occasion for me, as this was the first year that I had a job and was able to purchase gifts for all of my friends and I couldn't wait to splurge on each one of them. I looked forward to the day that I could return the blessing to Chris and Isabella in the same way that they gave to me. Isabella recently was terminated from her job at the doctor's office. According to her stepdad, the doctor's office investigated her visa status and found she didn't have one, so they had to let her go. She was in good spirits, considering the circumstances. She still managed to be online in purchasing clothes and purses. When I went to purchase Chris's Christmas gift, which was a shirt and tie, I included

Isabella's name on his card, as to say that she was a part of this gift purchase, although she wasn't. I didn't want her to feel left out. She had been too good to me, and this was the gesture I could give in returning the favor. I went to Macy's to purchase a specific shirt and tie with his accurate size and color. I observed Chris style and I knew in my heart that I hit the mark. I looked forward to him opening his present that came straight from my heart.

Chris came to pick Isabella up first, which I found odd, but I was too tired to understand that. I fell right to sleep in the back seat. When I woke up, Chris and Isabella were discussing how loud I was snoring. I came into the house still exhausted. Chris picked me up right after I worked. As I entered the house, I excused myself to go straight to the guest bedroom to sleep a little more. They let me sleep with no interruption. I woke up energized and ready to have a good time. I walked down to the living room to see that no one was in sight, not even in the kitchen. I heard some music downstairs in Chris's basement where he slept. I made my way downstairs to see the married couple slow dancing to some secular music and Isabella and Chris slow dancing like they were a couple. They didn't realize that I was standing right there, but when they noticed me there they all stopped dancing and we all headed back upstairs. Isabella and Chris decided that they wanted to stay behind to continue their conversation, which I respected. They were downstairs for a while when I walked back downstairs to see what they were talking about and if they were headed back upstairs. I slept most of the night and I was expecting us all to enjoy each other's company. On the stairs, I asked both of them when were they coming back upstairs? Isabella replied with an attitude like I was interrupting some deep conversation with deep secrets. Isabella brushed me off as if I couldn't hear what Chris was telling her. I knew Chris secrets so whatever they were discussing wasn't that much of a secret however I went back upstairs and waited for them to finish. It only took them a few minutes to walk upstairs, because Chris knew that I didn't play those types of games. They needed to get their act all the way correct. We all sat in the living room eating ice cream and a bowl of green grapes. As I sat there trying to talk and watch a movie, I noticed that something had changed in our dynamics. I tried not to give into bad energy or thoughts. It was weird because I kept feeling like I was getting ignored by two of my friends and they were gazing into each other's eyes, having their own conversations. But then I quietly walked out to the bedroom. It wasn't a big deal, which was why I didn't say anything to them, only removed myself from that type of atmosphere that bothered me. I had to be up in my room for ten minutes when Isabella came to check on me. I told her that I was fine, but you had to notice my body language, which apparently she did. She decided that she wanted to go ahead and go to sleep too. That was when the husband of the married couple came to talk to us. He encouraged us to never allow anyone, especially a man, to come between our friendship. He said that our relationship was too special for anyone to come in between that. We agreed and fell asleep.

The next day was Christmas and I was eager to exchange gifts with everyone, but more importantly, I was ready to share my gift with Chris. He had been like a big brother to me and I looked forward to his reaction when I handed him our gift. I cut the tag to Chris's shirt and tie and wrapped them nicely to present it to him. I walked down the stairs, excited to hand Chris his gift that I put a lot of thought and effort into. I had a specific budget for everybody else's gift except Chris. For Chris, I extended that budget so that I could purchase him something nice. Something I knew that he would love. He opened his gift with the both of our names on it and his eyes lit up. He thanked both of us and decided to go and try on his shirt and tie. Somehow Isabella accompanied him while he tried on his gifts which I thought was unnecessary but she had a sense of fashion and Chris wanted her to be there.

I headed down to his basement when I felt they were finished. They weren't. He was still in the shirt and she was examining his fit. Isabella was telling him to go back to the store to exchange the shirt for a different color and a different size and the tie didn't match. I couldn't believe what I was hearing and here Chris was falling for it. He agreed with her. I quickly got upset and felt like it was a slap in my face. I told both of them that nothing was wrong with the shirt and tie. It was all fine and he had to be okay with it since I no longer had the receipt and I trashed the tag. In my head, he was returning that shirt to please Isabella. I was so upset with both of them that I went back upstairs to go to bed. I was so over both of them. They were getting on my nerves. Isabella trailed behind me, trying to call her mother on her cell phone to come and pick her up, but there was a snow storm brewing that prevented her mother from driving thirty minutes to pick her up, so she had to stay and deal. We both went to sleep upset with each other. The next morning the men were outside shoveling the snow while we were inside the house making breakfast and hot coffee.

After the men finished shoveling the snow they came inside to eat breakfast and drink coffee. Following breakfast, Chris drove Isabella and me back to our homes. When Chris dropped me off at my apartment I had plans to distance myself from the both of them. For several weeks none of us really talked on the telephone. Then Chris called me to ask if I could join them to sing background at an African church and surely Isabella would be joining us. I didn't hang out with Isabella that often. I was still in my feelings, as she was too. Our personalities were similar in that we were strong-minded individuals. I assumed that Chris was trying to make up. When we got to the African church, they sat us down to eat and then we began to sing. After the singing, the pastor asked us to hold hands with the person standing closest to us. Isabella and I happened to be standing next to each other, so we decided to hold hands per instructions. I looked around, but there was nobody else seemingly close to me. The pastor asked us to repeat a prayer that we would stay connected to that person we were holding hands with, and hold each other accountable. That we would not depart from each other and build a relationship. How did this pastor know to pray about this type of prayer? God only knows what to have a man to say, because this was a defining moment for both of us. I appreciated the pastor for being obedient to the Holy Spirit to carry out a prayer like that. I left that church fulfilled, knowing that we would continue our friendship.

Chris called me on Isabella's birthday. He wanted to take Isabella to a Mexican restaurant since she never had their food before, and include a movie after dinner. He was going to treat and wanted me to join. I felt that it was a nice gesture to reconnect our friendships. I didn't hesitate to say yes to his invitation. Chris picked up both of us and it didn't matter that Isabella sat in the front seat. Chris opened the door for both of us as we entered the restaurant. I turned my head to see why they were walking slowly. Chris was embracing Isabella with a passionate hug as he missed her very much and it seemed to be a flirtatious hug. I thought to myself as I turned back around, "Here we go again." I sat down hoping this was not going to turn into another uncomfortable situation. Chris is old enough to be Isabella's grandfather.

Isabella found the food to be a delight, but she soon got sick and urged us to drop her back off at home. We did, and she told us to go ahead and go to the movies, which we did. When Chris and I hung out with just the two of us, it felt like the Chris that I adored. He was a different person when Isabella was around. Giving her a kiss on the checks when he walked her to the door and flirting. It was all inappropriate in my opinion and it made me feel uncomfortable. At the movies, I was in good spirits. As we headed out of the theater and he introduced me to his coworkers that he ran into, I knew in my heart and mind that I had to let go of our friendship in order to save my friendship with Isabella. I figured that Chris would be okay since he was a man and much older. I had Chris drop me off at Isabella's house. I walked in on her standing in her kitchen with lingerie on and the maintenance guy staring her down. Well, so much for her being sick. I only came by to check on her, but I could see that she was just fine, as she looked shocked when I walked in and then walked out.

Mrs. Irene invited me to meet her at one of her children's five-star restaurants, so I drove down to meet her. We sat there, me with my new big red Louie bag and a nice outfit that her grandkids' mother gave to me. I was taking this bag everywhere with me. Not only was it cute, but it was extremely convenient. So happy that I didn't save it for some TV interview. Instead, I was putting this bad boy to its proper use. Mrs. Irene then proceeded to hand me an envelope with a Christmas card and money in it, a few hundred dollars. She always blessed me just when I needed it. We finished our meal, which was scrumptious. She told me that I could stop by that restaurant anytime that I wanted, just tell them that I was her friend and the meal would be free every time. But I never went there unless I went there to meet Mrs. Irene. I thanked God for using Mrs. Irene to continue to bless me in my time of need. God never disappoints.

I felt that it was necessary to host a book signing of my own. I headed to my local library, where I read on the bulletin board about two local authors who were coming to share their books and holding their own book signing. I went to observe these two ladies, to hear them out and to learn. I entered this small room with the two authors sitting down facing their audience. There had to be about fifteen people in attendance. To the right of me as I entered the room was a table full of snacks and water. I sat down, listening to these two women. They were engaging with the audience as they read from their books. I walked away having confidence that I could do the same.

I set out on a mission to practice my poems in my apartment when I was not working and attending classes at Abundant Life Bible Institute. I had a plan. I asked one of the ladies who worked as a director at the kids' center where I volunteered if she could come to minister by praise dance. I had plans to have music and food there, just like the ladies did with a little extra. As I rehearsed my poetry, I began to wonder how it would be if I added passion and pain to the poems as I memorized them, to bring the poems to life and so that people wouldn't be sitting in boredom. Both of my books, Mercies of God and Life were about my life's journey with a lot of pain and happiness. I needed people to relate and feel that pain and know that we were overcomers by the word of our testimony. I was going all out for this book signing event even purchasing a new outfit to set the tone. I drove to the clothing store to find a dress that was within my budget. I walked straight to the sales rack. I got close to the rack and there was a light brown dress draped over. Almost like it was hanging on top of the sales rack, waiting and positioned for me. I lifted up the dress, which was my style, within my budget, and my size. I purchased it and skipped out of the store. I knew that God had placed that dress right there for me or the angels of heaven, somebody from heaven put that dress there. I love the Lord.

The night before the book signing event, I had to work my overnight job. I didn't have any money for gas to get to work that night, nor gum, and for the things that I needed for this event. But before I could let it concern me, I was on my cell phone, talking to my girlfriend, walking to my car parked in the parking lot across the street from my apartment building. While I was walking and talking, I walked right up to what looked like cash on the ground that met my feet. I bent down to see if my eyes were deceiving me. I picked up the money and unfolded it because it was tightly folded. When I unfolded the money, it was five crisp twenty dollar bills just lying on the concrete floor, waiting for me to pick it up. I couldn't stop laughing as I hung up the telephone with my dear friend, too excited to hang on. I shared my testimony and she was excited for me but I rushed to put gas in my car and to get a pack of gum. I quickly shared my testimony with my coworkers, as I was head over heels. I couldn't let a blessing like that stay within. I went to Walmart after my morning shift at work to pick up some snacks, water, and tablecloths and decorations. God met my needs and helped me to get prepared.

I went home to rest for a few hours, and when I woke up, I got my clothes together and went to pick up Pretty Eyes, who offered to help me decorate. I was happy to have my girlfriend beside me to help because she's skilled in making sure things were in order and neat. We argued during the course of her making sure that I was all set, but what was an event without a little drama? I changed into this proper brown dress and brown open toe shoes with matching stockings. I placed flyers around my town, posted on social sites, sent out hundreds of emails, and told some of my church members. I trusted that God would fill the seats. We had praise dancers of about ten ladies who ministered by mime also. Gospel music was playing in the background during our two breaks, and there were plenty of snacks, including fruit served to our guests. God sent about twenty-five people to sit in attendance at my first event. Some members of my church came, which was a shocking since I felt like they were strict with supporting people who didn't do much serving in the church. The guy who was choking in class after I prayed that God would choke him showed up. That was interesting, but he just sat there observing. The teacher whose church did my baptism was in attendance, and one lady who saw my flyer around town came by to show support. Pam even came through. Isabella finally showed up during the second half of my poetry reading. She showed up late, which was disappointing. Nonetheless, I was glad to see her there.

We all took pictures and I got to sign books. I must say that this event exceeded my expectations. While this was sort of my second event, I hadn't done one like this before. It was deep, heartfelt, passionate, and I didn't cry like I did the very first event at the Italian restaurant. This time I was prepared mentally, physically, and spiritually, and I gave it all I had. God prepared me by having me to sit down and watch two local women authors. Also I attended an event in New York with Pretty Eyes where there was live music, models, red carpet, and poetry being read. This one lady made me see that I can be stylish, sophisticated, attractive, and still be great while ministering my poetry. I knew in my heart that I had to minister my poetry again at a different location but at a different venue. This fire inside me only energized me to keep going.

Later I registered for an online book tour. It was the first time I had ever set up interviews on radio and blogs pertaining to my book. It was two months of radio and blog interviews. This was an exciting and exhausting time that I looked forward to every night. I had a good time being interviewed, sometimes back to back. There were over twenty interviews. One of my interviews asked me: Where would I like to travel? I answered that I would like to visit Israel to see the landmarks of where Jesus and His disciples walked and did His miracles, and Disneyland. My mother always wanted to take her children to Disneyland, but could never afford it.

I scheduled to take pictures at JCPenney. I needed pictures for my new website and flyers as I introduced my two books. JCPenney would take like three different poses for under twenty dollars. I went in a few days apart in different apparel, bringing in crops. I would take photos like I was at some photo shoot. The workers were gracious enough to allow me to take my time to take pictures to make sure they were good. I was on a roll and nothing could stop me from becoming all that God had planned for my life.

Discernment

I had been hanging out a lot with Pretty Eyes ever since she moved out of her auntie's house and back in with her mom. Her mom sold their house, and I helped them move out. I drove Pretty Eyes around and tried to spoil her as she spoiled me before. She would have her mother lend me a few bills until my next paycheck when I didn't have any money, usually because I had to get my car fixed. So I was sad when Pretty Eyes told me that God was moving her to Las Vegas. Why would God send a person who was recovering from sex addiction to a place that was considered a sin city? I was concerned for her and kept these thoughts to myself and just supported her with whatever she believed God was leading her. I never fought her beliefs, because you can't convince someone who told you that God told them what to do. It's a losing battle. You can only hope and pray that they heard God correctly, and if not, that God keeps them and helps them as they learn and grow.

Before she left New Jersey, I drove her through a part of Newark that was reminiscent of Oklahoma. She donated her van that her mother had given to her to our church, which they accepted. I drove Pretty Eyes past this park that's filled with trees, walking path, and water. It reminded me of the park Lake Hefner in Oklahoma that I walked around often with my family. The area had homes and apartments that I could see myself living in. I just fell in love with this area and I knew that God would make this place my home in the future. When we left her mother, I wanted to drive back through this particular neighborhood. We stopped the car to tour inside of a home that had a for rent sign. The owner of the property was already giving a tour to somebody else, and as they were walking out, we wanted a turn, so the landlord showed us his property, which was astonishing. I knew walking out that this was set. God would one day move me to this part of Newark. I didn't know when but I could see my future.

Pretty Eyes told me as she moved to Las Vegas that God led her to live in a shelter, however, it was unlike than the shelter that we attended together. Ultimately she wanted to start over in life. That was her goal, so she had high expectations as she traveled this road alone. The shelter was her obstacle, but she was determined to overcome and walk away unharmed and fearless. It was a rough season for my Pretty Eyes. All the circumstances of shelter living that appear on TV were Pretty Eyes' existence. She had to stand in line to enter the shelter building. She had to travel every day with her luggage. She had to sleep on dirty mattresses and bedbugs, with tons of people surrounding her. Eventually, the shelter moved her into one of those motels that had cockroaches and cigarette burn holes in the sheets. She talked to me every night over the telephone. I wired her a few dollars a few times, and her ex-husband sent her money along with her sister. Her money went towards her personal hygiene. She qualified for food stamps, so her food was a non-issue.

While transitioning and trying to find her way, she met a man who swept her off her feet by telling her sweet promises. She told me that she met the man God had sent to her. I believed her since she was convinced that this was heaven sent. She was swept off her feet until she fell back into lust and drawn to sin by fornicating. She had regrets, but this didn't stick true, as she moved into his apartment. I felt like Satan came when she was vulnerable by deceiving her. She was determined to walk the right path, and on her way, she was met by Satan's little brother. She told me how the first two weeks of living in his apartment, it seemed all good. He treated her like a princess, but it went downhill quickly. He became possessive, and in a matter of no time, he was controlling and monitoring her every move. She said that she slept next to him, and when she woke up she realized that she was sleeping with the enemy and his face looked like that of a demon. She had to wait for him to leave the apartment that they shared to risk sneaking out before he returned.

I believed that she learned all that she needed and was coming out even stronger. She left that man to become homeless again, staying all night at the twenty-four-hour McDonald's. I prayed all night with her and called my mother to pray with me that God would bless her out of this bad mess that she made for herself. And surely God came through like a flashing of light. Pretty Eyes told me the morning following our prayer that she was at McDonald's all night, not sure what to do when this stranger came to sit down next to her and talk to her about life. She said the gentleman was

Muslim, and after Pretty Eyes shared her struggle with him, this Muslim guy told her about a rich friend of his who housed employees. All they had to do was work for his business that dealt with sales and manufacturing. He would repay them by housing them in his mansion, that he had rooms specifically for his workers. He provided meals and he paid them enough cash to satisfy their needs. That night, Pretty Eyes trusted her instincts, which was the Holy Spirit, when this man asked her to come and sleep at his house over the weekend. He was married and his wife wouldn't mind. Thank God she went, because they welcomed her with open arms. She was fed and bathed and slept well. That Monday morning, this stranger drove Pretty Eyes to the mansion and introduced her to his rich friend. She was offered a job and shown where she would be sleeping. She would share a room with two other women. God turned her life around so quickly, just as the scripture says. Psalm 30:5, "For his anger endureth but a moment; in his favor is life: weeping may endure for a night, but joy cometh in the morning."

Pretty Eyes worked for a month, proving herself to the owner, and the owner promoted her to the lead overseeing the products and eventually overseeing the housing needs. She started attending a church where the church van came to pick her up. She met another man from the church she attended and this time she was certain that this man was sent from heaven. No, this time it was legit. She promised me. This guy was special in handling things slowly. They went on a few dates, but she tried hard not to end up as she had before, in some man's bed. She promised herself and God that she would no longer put herself in those positions ever again. I was happy for her and proud of how her journey had turned out. She set a goal, and Satan came to distract her and take her off course. She stayed in faith and my prayers and God's favor and forgiveness and patience transitioned her life in a short time. She went from sleeping in roach motels to a mansion and was promoted, riding around in a limousine courtesy of her boss, and she met a churchman who took it slow and respectfully. My God sure knows how to turn a situation around when we give Him control and finally let go, 2 Corinthians 12:9, " And he said unto me, My grace is sufficient for thee: for my strength is made perfect in weakness. Most gladly, therefore, will I rather glory in my infirmities, that the power of Christ may rest upon me."

Everybody wants a man and they're growing tired of waiting on God's plan and purpose for their life. They want God to speed it up and stop moving like a snail or turtle. God was moving too slowly. I tried to pray and talk to my Christian friends who were growing weary in well doing. Iron sharpens iron, and while I waited for what God had for me, I really needed my Christian brothers and sisters to do the same. I hoped that we could continue to hold each other accountable and lean on one another for inspiration, guidance, and friendship. To love each other while we waited and prayed for our faithful Jesus to come through as He promised. For the first two years, many were on board, but I could see that this was going to be hard for some to keep their promise.

When I talked to Isabella, it had been briefly due to our conflicting schedules. I was working and she was busy looking for work and shopping online for clothes and purses. Eventually, she got a job working for two children, when she had been looking for work for nine months. I came to her house looking forward to being in her presence, chatting it up as girlfriends do. I sat in her kitchen after she cooked us a home-cooked meal. This girl had hands like her mom in the kitchen. Her food was always filling. She truly knew a way to my heart. She fed me well and got me in a good spirit and relaxed when she popped the news to me that she had a new boyfriend. I was taken aback, as I didn't know that she had a boo. I was happy for her and urged her to share more as I sat inattention. I was listening with a bright smile. I was glad for my friend to find love that God sent to her. The way she talked about how sweet he was and that she'd been hanging out with him, going out on dates. She had a dream of the perfect guy proposing to her in all white. I was all for her love story. Listening to her made me hopeful that I was next. I was attentive as she grinned and shared their love. She shared with me how they met. She had been driving around town for weeks, being bored with nothing to do and trying to find herself. She would go into the twenty-four-hour donut store to evangelize to the people at 2 in the morning when one of those nights she met the guy. He was in there also.

Now, this struck me as kind of odd that she would be out so late at night. She went on to tell me that she and the guy talked, that she lost track of time, and they were talking past 2 am when their table began to shake. She said this was the sign of God, but I knew better. That entire story creeped me out. I told her no way that God was involved in this. For one, God doesn't want His child hanging out in the streets that late at night and early morning like that, and the fact that the table started to shake was not a good sign from God. I told her the table shaking was scary and God was trying to tell her to go home. I asked her if she had a picture of this gentleman, which she did on her cell phone. I proceeded to look at his picture and knew immediately by discernment that this guy was not the man for her and told her to ditch him. He was not this perfect specimen, she needed to run fast. She had a disappointed face after I spoke, but this was not a joke and I gave her time to dissolve this relationship. We continued to watch a movie. She hadn't let him go as days and weeks carried on, but I was still giving her time to let this matter go, like her friend who walked with her hand-in-hand like a spiritual partner. We were on this journey together, and like Jesus disciples', I needed her to act like one of them.

I drove to her house unannounced, as I always did. I went straight to her room and she looked uneasy as I entered her room. She was in full doll look with makeup and high heel boots and pretty outfit. She told me that she was going on a date to a bar in New York to watch a game, which explained the jersey that she was wearing. I thought that she broke it off with this dude. All of a sudden, my insides boiled. I was upset with her that she didn't listen and take what I had to say seriously. This was a serious matter to me, so much that I told her that I was ending our friendship and that we would no longer be friends. I walked out of her house with no intentions of speaking a word to her ever again. I meant what the heck I said. I could show her better than I could tell her.

The following Sunday she had the nerve to bring this fellow to our church play. Sitting in the same section where I sat, a row in front of me. He was filming the play like he was interested. I didn't speak to her or see her after this phony episode.

My friends were dropping out of my life due to them not wanting to wait on King Jesus to bring them their significant other. Oh, and how frustrating it was to watch my friendships end. April was another lovely young lady who I met during Impact Group from our church that I once attended with Chris every week when he and I were friends. April was the same age as me and her birthday was in the same month. When I met her, she had just broken off a five-year relationship that didn't end well. She was a hopeless romantic and was waiting for God to bring her "the one." She was just like me, determined to wait on the Lord to bring us the right man. She didn't want to rush it since she just came out of a serious and hurtful relationship. I could sympathize. April had a good head on her shoulders, with a good job, making a good income. She was very attractive with a great sense of style that complimented her natural beauty, and long black hair. She was the ideal woman for any man. Once a week we got to meet and we instantly gravitated to each other singing Christian songs and reading the word to God among our elders at the Impact Group. It had been months of April and I getting to know one another when she brought a new boo to church, standing next to her as I entered the sanctuary, waving as I pass her. When church service was over, April in her enthusiasm introduced me to her new man, who she met online. I knew the moment that I shook his hand, staring at his face, that this was not the man she was praying to God for. I could discern instantly that his spirit was not the right spirit and that she needed to run fast. I didn't know the spe-cifics of what he was hiding but I could discern that it was something terrible. This was going to be hard to tell April and bust her little happy bubble, but I had to tell her. It was like if a friend was in a house that was on fire. I had to try to get my friend out of the fire, otherwise, I would regret not saving that friend. I knew I had to tread lightly, as I didn't want to lose another friend, especially one I was not that familiar with. I was just starting this friendship and didn't want to be a bad person in her eyes.

I pulled her to the side and asked her new boo if I could borrow her for a moment. Once he said sure, I asked her if she had seriously prayed to God about their relationship. I told her that she should talk to God about him before going in so deeply and quickly. Immediately she answered me that she and her boyfriend prayed together about their relation-ship. She was sure that they had this under control and I was not to worry. She walked away holding hands with this character who was flawed. I needed God to help me deliver this message, so the following Sunday I had another mar-ried couple who I had met at Impact Group. They had met online. They had a strained relationship that wasn't doing well. I needed them to share their story so that this would put a light in April's heart and help her to reevaluate what she believed. Following church service, I asked this couple to come and talk to April and her new boyfriend. Maybe they could exchange phone numbers and talk more. This couple definitely shared pieces of their marriage and their struggle with April. I was hoping that April was listening.

The more I saw April with her man, Sunday after Sunday, sitting next to April's mom, the more I cringed. I could tell all over his face that she was playing with the enemy. I was also noticing it in his hair. Some Sundays he came to church looking like he was battling it out with demons and lost the fight. April's boyfriend seemed to try to defeat these hidden demons. I could tell he was coming up to the sanctuary for the altar call, but for some reason whatever demons he was fighting were a force to not be messed with if not by prayer and fasting. An indefinite period had passed and they still seemed like a happy couple having holidays together. I wondered if I discerned correctly. I doubted what God helped me to sense. I felt like I had to be wrong because Satan would have shown himself in a mighty way by now. Yet they were still walking and talking even about marriage. They were seeking marriage counseling through our church.

At this point, I gave up trying to deter her away in a subtle way. I felt like I was wrong or maybe things had changed, but I could see on his face that they didn't. Maybe I was seeing it wrong because he definitely did not fit the description of a man who was demonic. He dressed well and owned his own company as a personal trainer and drove a sports car. Even when he spoke he was a polite young man. His voice was pleasant and didn't match his face. He was ugly to me by what I was seeing of that demon. Just when I had moved on in not caring what they did, three steady and faithful years they were together had ended. They broke up and I could tell because they were sitting on opposite sides of the church. April confided in me during class that she and her boyfriend broke up. When I saw him, we talked, and he confided in me that he broke it off with her. I was shocked. He didn't tell her why, but he was battling some inner issues. I was blown away because everything that God had shown me came true. I asked him if he remembered when I told them to pray about their relationship and how I didn't think they were a match for each other. To my surprise, he remembered and asked me how I knew. I never told him, because the truth was that I was still trying to understand what gift God had given to me.

Instead of chilling and keeping quiet when I saw April, I told her about my conversation with her ex about them. She seemed okay with it. But then she stopped attending our church and never answered my calls. When we attended classes together, she would sit next to me and then switch seats, and never made eye contact. She wouldn't accept my friendship on Facebook. I was losing relationships because

I didn't keep silent. I would tell people what God had shown me. Maybe my delivery was harsh and a little too aggressive but this is where God would have to teach me, for God said in 1 Corinthians 1:27 & 28, "But God hath chosen the foolish things of the world to confound the wise; and God chosen the weak things of the world to confound the things which are mighty; And base things of the world, and things which are despised hath God chosen, yea, and things which are not, to bring to naught things that are."

Recover

Speaking of discerning Spirits, God was on a roll by using me. Ray, one of our church members who drove the church van. Before I had my car Chris or Ray would pick me up for the church, they switched Sundays. When I got a car I stopped riding the church van but sent out a group text of inspirational verses from the Bible. I liked Ray as he was a man who kept to himself but had a lot of baggage. He was getting his life in order with God and I paid close attention to him for some reason unbeknownst to me. Once I saw him driving the church van in my neighborhood, going down the wrong road. That road was not on his route. This area that he drove to was designated for drug dealers. Out of concern, I made Chris aware, who just assumed that Ray was out driving to evangelize. Chris said that the pastor was sending members out in two to minister to the people in the street. I couldn't recall seeing another person riding in the van with Ray. He seemed to be alone, however, I dismissed 'my thoughts, in hopes that Chris was right and it was nothing to concern myself about.

I was walking from my mechanic's, headed to my apartment when it appeared that Ray was walking inside the liquor store, so I followed him just to say hello. When he saw me he froze. I smiled and gave him a hug and asked how he was doing. He began to tell me that he was only in the liquor store because his roommates sent him. They didn't want to go, so they sent him. I didn't understand his need to tell me, although I thought the story that he told was a lie. I dismissed what he said because I didn't have a problem with Ray being in that place it wasn't my business and it didn't offend me. He asked me if I wanted anything out of the store like chips but I said no and walked out the door.

A few days later I drove to Walmart, and when I returned to my car it wouldn't start. I was frustrated and didn't know how to get back home, when lo and behold, here comes Ray walking towards Walmart, telling me that he was coming to get a movie. I told him that my car wouldn't start. He said that he would help me out. Ray got back in his car and pulled up behind mine to see what the matter was. As soon as he parked right behind mine and got out of his car, a lady backed up into his car, leaving a dent on his driver's side. This was amazing that he didn't get hurt but his side door was damaged. It was as if she didn't know how to drive and placed her feet on the gas and slammed into his car. I felt so bad for him because he was only parked so close to mine to help me out. Ray was in good spirits. He just said that his car was old and for the lady to continue on her day. Would you believe this lady drove her car forward, just to place her feet back on the gas to drive backward in our direction. That's when two tall black men who out of nowhere walked by, stopping her from banging into Ray's car again.

The reason why my car wouldn't start was that I was out of gas. The meter was broken, so I couldn't tell that it was on empty. Ray went and filled up a gas can to fill up my tank. I was relieved that it was not anything serious. Although, I worried about Ray as he headed home. I knew that he had been having difficult times. He told me that he lost his job by falling off of a ladder at the job. He took a job in New York and that job was not working out either. He was having a hard time and then a woman slammed her car into his. I was grateful that he stopped with all that was going on in his life. I also learned to go ahead and fill up my tank to capacity, instead of trying to save money by filling up halfway. It made more sense to do it the right way so that I wouldn't end up again in the same predicament.

Because Ray helped me, that made it hard for me to call the elder of our church when I saw Ray coming out again from the same liquor store at midnight. My spirit was grieved and upset. This matter upset me that it consumed my thoughts. I knew that I had to tell the elder of our church to save Ray from whatever he was going through. The Holy Spirit gave me this urgent sense and I had to roll with it. Up to this point, God never gives me the details, only enough to say what the Holy Spirit had revealed to me. I called the elder of the church to report what I witnessed and asked this elder to please have a conversation with Ray. I gave him the heads up that Ray would say that his roommate sent him, but that was a lie.

That conversation obviously happened, because when we both would go up by the sanctuary to praise and worship God, he would walk away. A few times I wanted to go and talk to him, but I could tell that his anger towards me was hot. He needed more time. Soon enough as time passed Ray and I would stand next to each other. He kept his distance, but I could tell that he was forgiving me when he smiled back.

I saw him walk out of the same liquor store at night for the third time. I knew that I had to go about this a different way. I didn't want to tell him, plus I learned in my class the appropriate way according to Matthew 18:15, "Moreover if thy brother shall trespass against thee, go and tell him his fault between thee and him alone: if he shall hear thee, thou hast gained thy brother. But if he will not hear thee, then take with thee one or two more, that in the mouth of two or three witnesses every word may be established. And if he shall neglect to hear them, tell it unto the church, let him be unto thee as a heathen man and a publican." Obviously, I did it wrong the first time by not speaking with Ray before going to the elder opening my mouth. This time during church at praise and worship, I went to ask one of the brothers in the church who I knew was overcoming hardships himself. I asked him if he could talk to Ray and be his friend without me doing any damage to Ray's reputation. This gentleman said yes. I led him over to Ray and introduced them to each other. They seemed to kick it off, talking, and I believe exchanging numbers.

A few months later I noticed that Ray was no longer at church and this worried me to the core. I asked the leader of the church van ministry, who told me that Ray had a car accident that involved drunk driving. He was banned from driving the church van and was sent to the church's rehab center. I was shocked because so much time had passed that I didn't understand why I had this strong sense. When it was revealed to everyone when I tried to warn Ray and the elder, I was satisfied in my soul that Ray was in rehab. I also thought about how brave of God to use me to help give Ray warnings. I'm sure that God had given Ray warning signs before I spoke but like many people, they ignore God's warnings so he has to send someone in their life to speak the truth. I never wanted to share his personal addictions as I wouldn't want anyone to reveal mines but this was a God thing. I would never get so upset seeing anyone come out of the liquor store but it was obvious that it was a deeper issue to the point of destruction. I just pray that Ray gives his life over to Christ Jesus and that Ray receives the help.

I walked into the cafe where I had been eating for years to order my usual. A half sandwich with a half salad. Sometimes I switched it up to order a pizza. Isabella's stepmother worked there as a cashier. We said hello, and while I was ordering my food she asked me if I had spoken to Isabella. Before I could say no, she told me that Isabella was at home recovering from being in the hospital. Her stepmother suggested that I go and visit Isabella, which I agreed to do. I hurried up and got my food to go. I went to the local dollar store to get a get well balloon and card and went straight to Isabella's house.

I walked in through her back door as if I was welcome. Her mother crossed her eyes as I went to see what the matter with Isabella was. I walked into Isabella's room. She looked at me with a mysterious look and asked me how I knew. I told her that a little birdie told me. I asked her how she was feeling, but we kept the conversation short. I didn't want to overdo it, but I wanted her to know that I still cared and I was concerned for her well-being. I left her house after giving her a hug and told her that I would come again to visit.

I made several trips to her house every week. Her sister and mother were cautious and standoffish. I'm sure that Isabella had nothing but negative things to say about me while we were not friends. I wasn't back in her life to have her family like me. My only focus was to make sure that Isabella and I were close again. I never want any of my loved ones to hurt, and the way I saw Isabella hurting crushed my soul. My only concern was to be here for her now. I was told that the owners of the house where Isabella's family lived found her on the floor because no one was there to watch her. I made it a point to watch Isabella while her parents worked during the day. Her parents would relieve me when they got home in the evening, then I would go to my apartment to rest before work that night. Her mother had a hot breakfast waiting for me on the stove when I came over in the morning and before I left to go to my apartment, she cooked me dinner. The only other thing that bothered Isabella's mother, besides the fact that the hospitals weren't able to find out what caused Isabella to faint and bleed, was that her stepfather was not working. This left all of the financial burdens on her shoulders. She often cried at night, and after I tucked Isabella in her room, I would sit on their living room couch for her mother to cry on my shoulder. The following day when I got paid, I gave her mother $40 to go towards fruit and any nutritional foods that Isabella would need. Isabella was on a special diet where she could only eat some fruits and eat soups, no other solid foods. Isabella was losing weight fast.

I went to work exhausted of watching Isabella every day. I couldn't keep up with not having proper sleep. Over the weekends, I spent the night over Isabella's house to be by her side. We would watch movies, laugh about silly stuff. I serenaded her with her sister's violin. I hadn't played the violin since a child in Elementary. It was humorous. At work, I slept during my break, which was something I took pride in not doing, but now was a different story. I was drained. On my break, I quietly went to the back room, shut the door and laid my precious head down on two chairs. My boss, who knew what happened to my friend, came to the back room, turned off the lights and allowed me to sleep for two hours.

My grandmother who adopted me into her family asked me if I thought that Isabella and her family would do the same for me since I am spending so much time at their house. My Grandmother didn't think that if the shoe was on the other feet it would be reciprocated. I argued with my Grandmother that surely Isabella and her family would look after me as much as I did for them. No doubt in my mind that they would give me the same treatment. After months of caring for Isabella, I did take my Grandmother's advice. Instead of going over Isabella's house every day I went twice a week. Isabella was getting some of her strength back where she could move around the house without hanging on to somebody else. Isabella's mother grew weary while Isabella waited to be called from a list of names to see a specialist about her health conditions. Isabella returned to the hospital on my birthday. I spent most of it in the hospital by her side, along with her other family members. But after a while, her family encouraged me to leave and to enjoy my special day. I gave Isabella a hug and took myself to the movies.

When Isabella returned home, she told me that she and her ex-boyfriend broke up because he had some anger issues. Isabella said that he had a fight in the bar and his mother warned her about him. I could see anger in the picture but didn't know what that meant. I wished that my friend heard my warnings. I just wanted my best friend to feel better.

Isabella's mother worked a lot of hours to save up money to send her daughter to Columbia to have the surgery that she should have received in the States, but the wait was for too long and they couldn't find out what was the problem. Her mother believed that by sending her to Columbia, the doctors would find a cure through surgery. I took Isabella to the mall to purchase items in the makeup department that she would need for her trip to Columbia. This girl surely loved her makeup. I lost track of time that was how long we were there. Nonetheless, I didn't complain, since I wouldn't see her for six months.

Isabella's mother said that the doctors in Columbia could do a better and quicker job with her surgery and she didn't have to be on a waiting list. I believed what her mother had faith in, and Isabella and I prayed together that it would all turn around for her good and that she would have an awesome testimony when she came out of this.

I stayed the night, lying on a pallet on the floor that her family made for me, and went with them as they drove Isabella to be sent off to Columbia. When we got to the airport, Isabella had to be wheeled in on a wheelchair. We all gave Isabella a hug and kiss and sent her away with lots of love. While my friend seemed weak and frail, I hoped and prayed that this surgery would be great. That she would recover well and come back better than ever.

While Pretty Eyes and Isabella were both away far from me, God gave me another assignment to start and finish. God placed it in my heart to host another poetry event, but this time in a community center in the center of the urban area. I was excited about this. Once Mrs. Irene heard about it, she volunteered to show support by financially assisting with every aspect of this event, even having one of her children who owned a five-star restaurant provide the food. Mrs. Irene handled my flyers, which came out amazing. Everything she did was exceptional. I had a DJ, food, praise dancers, and volunteers.

The day of the event, it didn't seem like many people were present, which made me get worried. The ladies who volunteered by greeting the guests and later helping supervise the food helped me say a prayer at the door that God would send more people through the doors and fill the seats, in Jesus' name. It hadn't been long after we said this prayer when many more people started to show up. The chairs were not filled, but it was enough for me to feel secure and to be content and happy. I shorted my poetry list, which made the event seem effortless. The praise dancers were fantastic and we had a singer. The food was superb and a surprise to the people. Mrs. Irene even had a florist to provide delicate flowers that sat on the tablecloth next to the provided food. I mean there was nothing short of amazing about my second major event.

CHAPTER EIGHT

Demonic Spirits

My pastor was genuinely passionate when he delivered the word of God. I tell you the truth that if it was not for my pastor, I would have uprooted myself. I had had my share of frustrations with the members of the church, however, like a blood family member, you have to stick with it unless it's detrimental to your health. I've come to learn that eventually, it all serves a purpose. Stay still and God will deal with each and every one of His children. I decided to stay where I was planted. I stayed where I was being fed the word of God so that I could apply the word of God to my daily life.

On Sunday my pastor commenced prophesying after preaching the word of God. Most of the prophecies were so good that when my pastor would go to a couple to prophesy over them I would stretch out my hands to receive. The words were powerful and ministered to my spirit as if my pastor included me in that prophesy.

I did this every Sunday that he prophesied over someone else's life. Sometimes I questioned in my heart if my pastor was making a mistake. The prophecy sounded so much like it belonged to me, like, "Pastor, I'm over here." Instead, I always just extended my arms and hands in agreement for that particular person but including myself in that prayer. Many Sundays and many prophecies were happening where I got to the point of being irritated, to the point when Pastor prophesied over a married couple as he walked down from the pulpit, I no longer wanted to take some else's blessing. I wanted mine. As I stood with the congregation, I realized that I needed to sit back down, and so I did. When my pastor finished prophesying over this couple, he walked back to the pulpit and continued to pace back and forth. Then the words that came out of his mouth that the Holy Spirit was not done. I knew that he was talking about me. I knew in my mind and heart that this time God had a message directly for me. I stood back up and waited to hear from the Lord. My pastor walked down from the pulpit towards my direction. I was about two seats away from the end of the row when the pastor extended his arm to me and prophesied about my life. A message sent from the Lord to my pastor's mouth to my ears. This prophesy gave me comfort, encouragement, and strengthened me to not only continue but that God was listening. My pastor walked away after a pretty long message and I was satisfied in my spirit.

God inspired me that I decided to take a class on demons and evil spirits that my pastor was teaching. I had a full schedule with working overnight, the books, and events, but attending these classes meant the world to me. I was a changed woman when it came to education. When I was a child in Middle School and High School I skipped school almost every day that I don't know how I passed to the next grade. When I did go to class I sat in the back of the class not paying attention. But now that I'm walking with Christ I cared about life. I take education seriously and appreciate the opportunity to learn, 2 Corinthians 5:17 & 18, "Therefore if any man is in Christ, he is a new creature: old things are passed away; behold, all things become new. And all things are of God, who hath reconciled us to himself by Jesus Christ, and hath given to us the ministry of reconciliation;"

The demon class was an evening class and the class was on nights I was off from work. I was driving when my car was having trouble. It completely stopped on me on the road. It was a good thing that I was still in my neighborhood to take my car to my mechanic. When I went to my mechanic nothing seemed to be wrong with the car, although it just stopped on me in traffic. I shook my head in disbelief and drove to class. I knew that God would safely get me to my class, but now I was running late. I eventually made it to the class about twenty minutes late, which I disliked. Instead of walking to the front of the class not to disturb the flow, I sat in the back of the class.

Our class was held in the back of our church in one of our other buildings. When you entered the classroom there was our pastor standing in the front speaking. I entered the class-room as quiet as possible and sat in the back where there were a couple of random chairs and tables that didn't go with the flow of the classroom set up. The students were facing our pastor with an aisle that separated half of the students in attendance to make room for the pastor to walk up and down. Sitting in front of me were two couples sitting on the right of me. One of the couples I recognized as members of the church. The other couple I did not recognize. The couple that seemed not to be members stood out to me because the woman stood up and went outside. When she returned, it seemed that she had gum in her hands. She placed a piece in her mouth and then she extended a piece to her husband. While the pastor was teaching, this lady kept moving in her seat, not being settled. All of a sudden, while the pastor was teaching on demons, her chair flew all the way to the back where I was sitting, and she ended up next to me while she was still in the chair.

My pastor stopped teaching to rush to the back. He prayed over her while the other students extended their hands to pray for her. Now I, on the other hand, was shocked. What I was witnessing, I had never encountered. I had only seen this type of situation on TV. By, how she was acting, she seemed to have been possessed by demons. I mean, she had no control over her movements, like something else was inside her, making the decisions for her. I tried to pray for her like the others, but really I was staring, just not moving, but watching her in shock. My pastor prayed over her for a while and then he stopped and we then took a break.

When Pastor left, I think he left the building, everyone walked around, talking. Some of the ladies stayed with the woman who seemed to be possessed, asking her if she was okay. I went to the restroom, and when I returned, I just kept saying that I never experienced this before, while others said that this was nothing new to them. I went closer to the woman while we were still on our break and others talked. I rubbed my hands on her arm to comfort her and to show sympathy. But when I rubbed her arms, she moved my hand off her in anger, like, "Do not touch me." I knew that not all of the demons had left her body. She had too much attitude off of me rubbing her arms for them suckers to have left her body. But what was I to do? I had never encountered nor experienced this before, so I kept my distance. My pastor ended the class sooner than usual and invited this young lady and her husband to come back to see him at a later date in private so that they could continue their session. When the pastor left the building the rest of the students left as well. We all left kind of amazed at what we just witnessed. I drove home in deep thought. When I arrived at my apartment building I laid down with my Christian music on. I was exhausted as if I had done some work. Praying for someone with demons was exhausting, and to be honest, I wasn't even doing that much praying. Maybe being in that type of atmosphere wore me out. I had a good night and was ready to fall asleep. I could only imagine how tired our pastor was since he was the one who did the work of casting out those demons.

While I laid down, trying to go to sleep, I could hear movement outside of my doors, which was on the stairwell. I could hear footsteps coming up and down the stairs. It continued all night like demons were on the steps of my apartment building with nowhere to go but hunt my stairwell. I eventually confided in someone, who said that the demons had followed me home. Thank God that I was protected and the evil one could not enter my apartment. By the blood of Jesus, I am always protected. God said the devil cannot touch the hairs on my head. I have angels of heaven protecting and guarding me twenty-four hours of the day so I have no fear and I rebuke those demons in the name of Jesus. Amen

The demonology class was enlightening. Some of the elders questioned why the pastor would have such a class, especially due to us witnessing a demon-possessed individual and what was happening to her. The lady who was possessed by demons continued to show up for class. We all gave her room and space to breathe, to take on the class. We were all there to learn and grow. I hadn't heard the demons in my stairway again, but the demons were not finished coming against me. Other than feeling like Satan using Princess, my other neighbors had shown me respect and distance. I could happily come to a quiet home with no sense of anyone bothering me. By this time, my neighbors were used to me not speaking. They would see me coming in and out. I was never around to hang out and socialize inside or around my apartment building.

My one neighbor who was a young fella once spoke to me when he first moved in. When he noticed that I didn't speak back, he didn't bother to speak to me again. He minds his business and kept it pushing as I did the same. My young neighbor was pretty much quiet as well. He went to work and came home in silence. Which was why I found it odd when I got off the elevator after my class to see about five men standing outside his door in the hallway, talking loud. As I passed by these men, who made a path for me to walk past them, one of the men who wore dreadlocks spoke to me, which I ignored. I could hear my neighbor say to him, "Oh she doesn't speak."

I could see at the corner of my eye, as I was opening my front door, the man with the dreadlocks had followed me to my apartment and had this awkward, conniving grin. That night I fell asleep listening to my Christian music from my radio. I could hear a person outside my door say, as I slept, that they knew how to unlock these types of locks. I quickly opened my eyes, leaped out of bed, and ran to my front door. I could hear two sets of feet dash away from my door, open the door to the stairwell, and run down the stairs. Thank God that He allowed me to hear the plans of the enemy even in my deep sleep. I was awakened and no harm was done to me. Satan had a plan, but God did not allow him to fulfill his desire to harm me.

I called the police, who said that they would watch out in the neighborhood and speak with my landlord about the video cameras. Well, my maintenance man informed the police and me that the video cameras were not operational. That didn't last long, because I noticed more cameras around the building seemed to be working and displayed in the elevator.

The next day, I walked to the elevator to stand behind one of my neighbors, who I couldn't tell if it was a boy or girl. When I squinted, this person looked like a girl, but dressed and had the demeanor of a boy. This neighbor would play secular music so loud that once I realized she was playing the same station I was listening to. At this point in my life, I was sneaking to listen to more secular music that's not good for the ears but I was getting tired of hearing the same gospel and Christian songs. But when I heard this neighbor and me playing the same type of music at the same time, I switched my station back on the gospel radio station. I made a vow to myself that as long as I lived in that building, my radio station would stay on my inspirational stations.

I stood behind her while she waited for the elevator. She looked back. When she saw me, she walked away in a hurry like she seen a ghost. The elevator had arrived and I yelled for her to come back but she rushed down the stairs as her life depended on it. At that moment God then revealed in my spirit the two people who were trying to open my door was the man with the dreadlocks and the person who said to themselves that they could open these types of locks was that she-man. It made perfect sense why she would rush out of my sight, Deuteronomy 20:3&4, "And shall say unto them, Hear, O Israel, ye approach this day unto battle against your enemies: let not your hearts faint, fear not, and do not tremble, neither be ye terrified because of them; For the LORD your God is he that goeth with you, to fight for you against your enemies, to save you."

Demonic Spirits were trying my life during my demonology class. I was on the elevator, coming from class, going home to rest. This tall, black, thick lady was standing in the elevator with a gentleman, who entered the elevator at the same time as me. Now I recognized this woman because she often came to visit that apartment that was on the first floor that host the parties every weekend. Well, this lady never spoke a word to me until we were in the elevator. Out of nowhere, she called me a bitch, while I didn't say a word to her. She looked as if she wanted to slap the taste out of my mouth. I just looked at her trying to not take offense to this stranger calling me out of my name. The man who she was with didn't say anything. I got off the elevator on my floor, not knowing what to do about that encounter. I called my mother and sister who calmed me down. My sister told me to just ignore this lady. I took my sister's advice. Satan was using this lady to attack me verbally. I saw this lady more often after our elevator incident. God is good because the times that I did see her there was a police officer right on the outside our building.

A few weeks later there was an event happening in the park on the green. There was a well-known praise dancer to come out and speak. There were plenty of praise dancers in the park this particular day, and after this event, they marched to a local church to continue the happenings. As they were taking the offerings, we had to stand up and go up to the front of the altar to hand in our offering in the bucket. As I was walking back to my seat, I saw the lady who insulted me in the elevator, looking like she was alcohol-free and on her best behavior. I didn't know if she recognized me, but she was there, acting as if she was a child of God. I found this entertaining to witness a lady who got drunk often and cursed random people out on the elevator, now dancing to the gospel music and walking to the offering bucket.

During my demonology class, although learning new things I was having dangerous episodes. At night, close to 7 pm, I was walking from CVS towards my apartment building. There were plenty of folks standing outside, out on the corners, pedestrians walking, and plenty of cars driving by. I passed a young man who was with two other young men, but there were plenty of other men around. As I was passing him, I could see that he motioned by nodding his head as a signal to follow me. I saw that. So to make sure that I wasn't going crazy, instead of walking straight towards my apartment building, I made a quick decision to turn left and to walk across the street. The three men followed a few feet away from me. I kept walking, knowing they were following, so I came to a complete stop right in front of a church. I turned to face the oncoming traffic on the street, to allow the men to pass me. There was plenty of street light. I stopped, and in a few seconds the three men walked past me and my eyes followed them.

I asked God that if these men meant me harm, to please have them turn around as they continued to walk cutting the corner. So the man that motioned for the other two men to follow me, well he looked back after my prayer. He turned back around to keep walking. I asked God again if these men had plans to do harm to me, please allow them to look back again. So the leader of the pack, he turned to look back at me and we made eye contact. Then he turned to look forward to keeping walking. I asked God a third and final time that if these men were truly going to harm me, to please have them look back again, so the guy who looked back the other two times looked back again. This time he seemed angry and irritated. As he turned to look at me, I was looking at him, making eye contact. In amaze, I just thanked God for keeping me safe, once again keeping from the plans of Satan.

A couple of nights after this I came home from another night of demonology class, drained and ready to hit the sack.

I entered the building to see and hear the black man with dreadlocks, who tried to break into my apartment, facing a Caucasian lady, screaming at her. He was just going on and on. I was planning on taking the elevator, but when I saw that he was there with this lady, waiting on that same elevator, I changed my mind. I wondered what to do, so I decided to take the stairs. He wouldn't know that I was there since his back was towards me. I crept past him, but as I was doing so, I could see the woman trying to get his attention to turn and look my direction. The man was so into his screaming at her that he didn't budge to turn in my direction.

As I'm walking towards the stairs I see nosey neighbors peeking their heads out of their apartment. When I made it to the stairs, I hurried up the stairs until I got to my door. I quickly opened it. As I locked it, I could hear the elevator arriving on my floor and the angry man yelling at this lady entering my neighbor's apartment. I kept my lights off and called the police for a disturbance. The police officers arrived at my apartment building in the nick of time. I could hear the two men standing right outside my door, talking among themselves, while the lady was in the apartment with the policemen. I stood in my apartment quietly praising Jesus like yeah Satan you going down tonight.

The next few days, my neighbor ignored the man with dreadlocks when he came knocking on the door. I knew because I would hear him knocking on the door and yelling, "I know that you're in there." The man with the dreads would sometimes take the stairs, but wait to see if my neighbor was coming out. My neighbor would eventually come out when he knew this man was long gone. I assumed that my neighbor wanted to have nothing to do with cops coming to his apartment. Eventually, this man with dreadlocks stopped coming to our building. He didn't know that I called the police on him. He probably thought the neighbor did it. His friend. Oh well, not my problem. I couldn't have been happier when this criminal man vanished.

I Give Unto You Power to Tread on Serpents and Scorpions

My job was a blessed and safe place for me. I went from not working and living on government assistance to working for a company that serviced the rich and famous. I felt fortunate and blessed to be among them on a daily. I never took that for granted. Many of them were gracious when they tipped. Normally the type of position that I held didn't require a customer to tip but I always got tipped large amounts of money. God made this job for me. My job hosted a wedding and I looked forward to seeing beautiful brides entering our facility with their handsome groom visioning that will be me sooner than later.

I often got tipped which covered my gas and food when I was short from paying my rent. I was late on rent most of the months but my Landlord didn't pressure me to pay on time. I don't know another Landlord who didn't make you pay for the late fees. He seemed to work with me since I was working with him living in that filthy and disgusting apartment. Had God shown me the entirety of the grossness in the very beginning I would have not moved in. I was just happy to move out of the shelter into my own place. Since I didn't shower every day like a normal person I was grateful to take long and much-needed baths at my job when I spent the night.

My co-workers and I got along which helped since we worked some nights more than eight hours a day for years. At first, the road was rocky, and then we grew to respect each other. I clashed with quite a few workers, but at the end of the day, we were all there to work and not make friends. My immediate Overnight Manager Katherine was one who had a snappy and grouchy personality about herself. Many times it was a struggle to work with her. She would snap at me for no reason, a few hours later she would want me to come back to her office to have a casual conversation like she wasn't just rude. Katherine's attitude needed adjusting but one of her positive attributes was that she was a dedicated and hard worker. Which is probably one of the reasons why she never got fired from all the complaints that people had made on her. I must say that after about three years of working with her and our team we began to have an understanding as to how to communicate with one another. We no longer took offense to what we said to each other. Finally, we were able to defuse our arguments and become stronger as a team. We had a rhythm that was working out for us.

I had been working for our company for three years, Katherine five years and our bellman eight years. There were many new faces that came in and out however we stayed and that was big for our company and for our guest who didn't like to explain themselves. They liked that we knew what they liked when we saw their faces.

When our new security guard Edward came on board we acknowledged him with a smile and tried to get to know him since he's a part of the Overnight team. Edward initially was polite and seemed to desire to thrive in his position. What caught my attention about him at first was that he had pearly white, straight teeth with a beautiful smile. He told me that he used to have long dreadlocks, I couldn't imagine it, because he didn't seem like a man who had dreadlocks as a hair choice. In my mind, I just couldn't see it. He went on to say that he had a woman who he was with for over twelve years. The way he spoke about her and they're living together, and the fact that I had mentioned that I was a Christian, I assumed that he was married due to the flow of our conversation. He told me when we were getting to know each other that he used to be a bouncer at a nightclub. He said that he once threw a couple out of the nightclub naked when he found them in the bathroom, knocking boots. I looked at him like, what in the world did you just reveal to me?

He went on to say that he once threw a man against the wall at the nightclub, leaving a dent. I thought, "This man seems to have some type of anger issue, but that will not fly at this establishment. You have to be nice and gentle with our clientele." Not only would they sue, but our company would not stand for that kind of behavior and assault. I hoped that he would work out just fine, besides all of that had happened in his past. He seemed like a nice dude like we would get along. We were getting along just fine so far.

It didn't take Satan too long to appear out of Edward. Quickly Edward was showing a crazy side. One of the younger security officers told me in private that Edward yelled at him and then hit him on the hand hard. I wanted to stand up for this young security officer to report this to HR, but I was told not to say anything. Well, this didn't sit well with me and it was definitely an incident that I kept in the back of my head. The younger security officer was one who was polite and stayed to himself. I couldn't stand bullying. I thought that Edward was going to work only the Overnight shift but he was working both the morning and evening shift. I didn't see him as much as I did when he first got hired which was good especially since I heard about his bullying.

This particular night we were going to be busy so Edward was scheduled to work the Overnight shift. Usually, the guest would get out of hand with drinking too much and partying over the weekend and for a wedding. It was to be expected. I heard a man yelling at the top of his lungs, so I went out from the front desk to see what the commotion was all about. I found it strange that Katherine didn't budge. Before I could move closer to the guest and Edward, they were exiting the bar, heading to the lobby. Edward was the one yelling at the guest like a mad man. He obviously didn't get the memo of how to properly treat our guest which rubbed me the wrong way. I stared at him, while Katherine was mum as if she wasn't the Manager. Once they ended up in the lobby, Edward tried to downplay his role in humiliating the guest and coming across as some evil lunatic that would be unemployed in about 2.5 seconds. I was just in disbelief because we never argued with a guest. The way they ended the argument was Edward made the guest feel like it was his fault. I never heard such a harsh tone full of anger towards a guest. It was not only disappointing but disturbing, to say the least. I didn't think that this guest would file a complaint since he seemed to be intoxicated. He probably wouldn't even remember or think that it the next day.

The morning that we were clocking out and leaving work to go home, I went to clock out and present my purse to the security guards before I left the building, as I was instructed. That was when Edward demanded that I leave the post and never enter the security office again. His tone towards me was harsh and rubbed me the wrong way. It kind of reminded me of him being a jerk to the guest. I surely had enough of Edward and was willing to show him. His next words had me react so that we were now arguing in the security office.

He seemed to want to lay his hands on me and he told me that he would. Well, the good Lord rose up in me like I matched the size of this tight end NFL-looking dude. I placed my fingers in his face, rolled my neck sternly, and told him what he was not about to do to me. Katherine was standing right in the middle, not interfering like the cat got her tongue and she didn't dare try to control this situation.

The very next day, HR had to get involved. They had no choice but to hear about it because the heated argument that seemed like it was about to break out into a fight happened in the security office. I just happened to walk away in my anger. The Director of Operations had a brief conversation with me regarding Edward and I. The Director said that Edward told HR that I cussed him out. The Director told me that when he heard that he knew that Edward was lying. The Director said that he told HR that he's seen me upset and in all the years I have worked under him that he's never heard one curse word come out of my mouth. Edward got fired, and later Katherine quit.

I got home and went to sleep. In my dream, there was a room full of people and some of the faces I recognized as workers at my building. I was walking away from a lady who was hovering over all of our bodies as she was administering voodoo. She couldn't do the voodoo on me because I ran to the nearby restroom and hid in there. I woke up feeling like somebody just tried to do voodoo on me but God saved me. God said that Satan could not put his hands on me. God protects me from the hands of the enemy, Luke 10:19, "Behold, I give unto you power to tread on serpents and scorpions, and over all the power of the enemy: and nothing shall by any means hurt you."

In my heart, I believe that the woman who was hovering over my coworkers and trying voodoo on me was Edward's girlfriend. I just have this strong sense that it was her, Isaiah 54: 17, "No weapon that is formed against thee shall prosper; and every tongue that shall rise against thee in judgment thou shalt condemn. This is the heritage of the servants of the LORD, and their righteousness is of me, saith the LORD." In that moment of believing that it was her, I prayed that she wasn't able to accomplish this voodoo witchcraft on my coworkers and what the enemy had planned might not touch us but turn around and go back to that individual.

I bumped into Sammy at the local Walmart as I was entering. She got me up to speed on all of the news of our old co-workers at the hotel where I used to work. She asked me if I heard about Sophia. I told her that I had not. She went on to tell me that Sophia had died. She apparently committed suicide. I was surprised, as I didn't see her as a person who would ever think about doing this. The last I knew she also had little children. It broke my heart that the rack hanging in the back of me broke my fall. Sammy and I concluded our conversation and I walked around Walmart disoriented. When I got to my apartment, I just cried knowing that I didn't try hard enough to reach out to Sophia when I had the opportunity. I was disappointed in my lack of being able to attempt to be a friend to Sophia. I thought that I had later to communicate with her but later would never be an option for me and this revelation hurt me to the core.

I began to miss my closeness with Pretty Eyes and Isabella. I needed them back in my life more than ever. They were truly missed. Pretty Eyes was still out of town, trying to figure things out. She said that God was calling her to move back to New Jersey. I couldn't wait for her return. Isabella and I weren't talking as much, which at first kind of hurt my feelings, but I knew that she had to recover in her own way. I needed to let her heal how she saw fit. We were still friends, but I thought that we would talk more often and I think we talked once a month. Her time to return home from Columbia was coming soon and I couldn't wait to hear her story and reconnecting. I went to her house every week, just to check on her family to make sure they were doing well. I stayed for as long as I wanted while Isabella was gone in her house watching movies and still eating good food. Her family actually encouraged me to continue to come over and relax as often as my heart desires.

Isabella didn't tell me exactly what was wrong with her. She mentioned a trace of cancer but we never had an in-depth conversation about it. I didn't pressure her to tell me what was going on with her body. I kind of wanted her to share when she was ready. Her surgery went well, and she would be returning home before the six months was up.

Until my friends returned home, God kept me busy. My job volunteered at different organizations. Since I left the shelter, I had the heart and desire to give of my time to volunteer. However, I couldn't find the perfect fit. My job volunteered at a food pantry that was not far from where I lived. Once I found this out I knew in my heart right away that I should volunteer with our team. When I stepped foot on the premises of the food pantry I knew that the pantry would be the place where I continued to volunteer even outside of my job. Mrs. Irene and other volunteers who I met along the way has left a grateful impact on me where all I want to do is give back, Proverbs 19:17, "He that hath pity upon the poor lendeth unto the LORD; and that which he hath given will he pay him again." Matthew 25:35 & 36, "For I was hungry, and ye gave me meat: I was thirsty, and ye gave me drink: I was a stranger, and ye took me in. Naked, and ye clothed me: I was sick, and ye visited me: I was in prison, and ye came unto me."

It's a nice feeling to volunteer. The feeling of fulfillment is not matched to any other feeling in this world. It's a life-changing. The ones who are receiving the help is blessed surely the ones giving the blessing is blessed as well. Not even the craziness of my new neighbor in my apartment building who lives on my floor placing mice traps in the hallway could discourage me on this journey. I did call the houseman and Landlord to report it. I mean when I was walking out of my apartment I would walk pass mice that were trapped on traps. To make matters worst the traps would be in the same place for a couple of days which meant the lady who was supposed to clean our building every day wasn't doing her job. And then I noticed that the mailroom started to pile up with trash and debris. I was scared to walk in our mail area to retrieve my mail. I kept calling the management company to make complaints.

My new manager Ricky who had taken Katherine position was a pretty cool boss. He was not uptight, argumentative, and rude like Katherine. He was just the opposite. He had two full-time jobs and a wife. Ricky was a heavy-set dude who liked to eat a lot. He was my eating buddy and made sure that I got extra free snacks from our sundry shop next to our front desk. He slept a lot during work, like three to four hours. I fell asleep only on occasion at work. I fell asleep during my break for an hour. I went to the front desk once I woke up, to finish my workload. When I went back to the chair where I was napping in the back office, I could see a small bug on the desk. It appeared to be a bed bug. I went online to do some investigating and sure enough, it was a bedbug but I didn't know how that appeared there. Goodness, I hoped that it wasn't bedbugs in my apartment and on my clothes. I quickly killed that bug, in hopes that Ricky didn't see it. I would have been embarrassed if Ricky saw it. He didn't say anything to me. I really hoped that God wouldn't allow me to be embarrassed like this. My maintenance man asked me not that long ago if I had noticed any bedbugs in my apartment because some of the other tenants complained about it. When he asked me I told him no because I never saw one but now that I saw one at my job on the desk where I took a quick nap oh now I had to go back to my apartment to search on my beds and walls. In my apartment I tried to wipe down my mattress and keep my clothes off of the bed and on the clothes rack that was near my bed.

CHAPTER NINE

God's Disciple

Mrs. Irene shared with me that she had been sick. When she went to the doctors in New York, they told her that she had cancer. Mrs. Irene said that she would be in recovery for a while and didn't want any visitors. I wouldn't be able to see her for a while. I had two friends recovering from cancer. I was crushed when Mrs. Irene told me this dreadful news. I not only had Isabella recovering but now Mrs. Irene from the same disease. This was too much for my mind to handle but I had to be strong and there for my two good friends. It was my turn to give back to them as they did for me in my time of need.

On my way to the Property Management office to pay a portion of my rent in cash, as I had been doing for three years. One of the managers whispered in my ear to make sure that I saved my rent receipts. Recently they had to take a tenant to court about this, and the tenant said the management lost their rent receipts. I nodded my head in agreement but walked away knowing that I had not saved my rent receipts. I knew that I had to start saving my rent receipts pronto. I was putting too much trust in the people. Thank God that I received a heads up because it didn't take too much longer after this conversation for the management office to send me a letter that I owed money for some months. Because I received the heads up, I had the rent receipts in question. I knew one thing for sure: I did not want to suffer the consequences of another eviction. I already went through that once before and I was not looking forward to enduring that again.

I always compared my life during these trying times to the life of Joseph in the Bible. He was unfairly placed in the ditch by his brother. He was lied to several times, put in prison, looked over and forgotten. I waited for the day when I would be sitting high in God's glory. I looked forward to a different type of blessing. Until then, I would sit still, continue to be patient, and wait on the LORD and allow God to justify and fight my battles and bring me out when it's His time.

It had been six months since Isabella had left New Jersey to travel to Columbia and here she was returning back home. I'll never forget that time I needed a friend when God told me to call my best friend, wondering what to do for the Fourth of July. He was telling me to call Isabella and I did. We ended up having the best of time.

Isabella and I shared a special bond. We were connected not only in the natural sense but the spiritual one as well. I could see both of us going into ministry together and I shared this with Isabella multiple times. We could be like God's disciples, how He separated them by twos to go out to minister. We would be a dynamic team. I knew that we had to continue to be obedient and patient. I could see that our friendship was strong. While I had all of these plans for us I knew that I had to move slowly.

When Isabella arrived back home, I had taken Isabella and her sister to the cafe restaurant where her stepmother worked at to eat s'mores and drink hot chocolate, we then went to a nearby park to walk and talk. Isabella shared with us her time in Columbia. She told us that her surgery was painless and she healed quickly. The doctors were supportive and made sure that she recovered fully before she returned to the States. She was enthralled with the atmosphere, which was surrounded by mountains and plenty of trees. She met a cab driver who she ministered to. She came to find out that he was a brother in Christ, so he invited her to his church.

She went to his church every Sunday. She also met a veterinary physician who lived in the same condominium building as her auntie, where Isabella was residing. He planned to come to visit New Jersey in the near future, so her mother invited him to come and stay in their home when he came.

The next few days of Isabella's return back home, her Bible study crew came by to visit her sometimes in groups, bringing her gifts and flowers. Isabella posted their gifts on Facebook with a generous paragraph of appreciation. I had been there for her, doing so much and I brought her a card, but she didn't mention me in her appreciation not even once. I felt offended so I brought this to her attention. The next thing I knew she posted a comment about me on her Facebook account but not until I brought it to her attention. I could see that she was taking me for granted.

She went to her Bible study every week with her new group of young adults. I was sincerely happy for her. I always wanted her to be around people her age. We were about five-year difference and although she was mature for her age, she needed to be around people her own age. I felt like it would give her a nice balance in life.

Eric, one of her Bible study friends, a young man who was handsome to include a nice gentleman came by Isabella's house faithfully on Sundays to take her to church. Isabella couldn't drive until she was able to regain her strength. Isabella showed me a picture of Eric and I immediately gave her the two thumbs up. I could tell by his picture that he had nothing but good intentions. He was a God-fearing man. I approved of Eric than any other guy she had been attracted to.

Her Bible study friends was a young and vibrant crew. They went out to many places. Isabella would share with me the time they went to Medieval Times. One of their members was getting married and Eric came to pick up Isabella to attend the wedding. Isabella was surrounded by all of this young love. Most of her Bible study members were in committed relationships within the group there were several couples which influenced Isabella to pursue the same. We didn't go to the same church, therefore, we weren't as close as we were before. I still came over to her house to sit and eat. I recognized that when she made me a plate that she didn't make her one. She just sat at the table not engaging in conversation yet she was on her cell phone.

Immediately upon Isabella's return, her mother urged her to find a job. Most of Isabella's friends from her Bible study had great paying jobs. Isabella wanted the same things in life as they did. It seemed the full-time ministry with me was behind her. She was uninterested whenever I mentioned it, but I kept the hope alive in my heart.

I had taken Isabella on a few job interviews. She didn't want to go back to the job that she held working with a family and watching their two children. She wanted to get back into the medical field. One evening I went to Isabella's house looking for her when her stepfather told me that she went out of town with Eric and some of his friends to Philadelphia. She spent the entire day with them. The next day, I spoke with her about her trip. She told me how free she felt being away from the pressures of getting a job to be in an element of total relaxation. Eric was a gentleman during their trip. I was relieved that Isabella found a good guy. I kept missing him whenever he came to visit her. For sure I wanted to meet him.

Isabella had a job interview. I gave her one of my black blazers since she had no interview clothes. Following that interview, Isabella accompanied me to my church for a Thanksgiving dinner. This was the first year where they had Thanksgiving dinner catered for the church members. Isabella and I dressed our best, looking cute, confident, taking pictures and enjoying each other's company. I love this girl. It seemed as if everybody was glad to see Isabella since they hadn't laid eyes on her for years. The last that they heard from her was when she got sick. I had lots of people praying for her. I even went to the altar call when they were praying for sick people. I went on behalf of Isabella. I wanted that girl to be healed.

Isabella and I walked around her house praying, speaking in tongues, and lifting up the name of the Lord. I laid hands on Isabella's stomach for a speedy recovery and for that illness to never return. I also went to her house, laying my hands on the bedroom doors, praying for peace and rebuking the enemy. Isabella's mother was growing anxious for her to find a job, ASAP. She was frustrated with almost everybody in the house. Her stepfather couldn't find work for over a year, so he began to drink often. The arguments would be so aggressive and intense that Isabella's stepdad would sleep in the basement. Isabella would complain, calling her stepfather a lazy bum. She spoke critically of him and judged his every move. I found myself giving him the benefit of the doubt. I saw him as a hurting human being. A man who couldn't make things work out yet he was trying. No one seemed to care and acted cruelly towards him. I found it odd that Isabella didn't show compassion given her circumstances. I would think that she would treat him better but she was acting like her mother.

Her mother would wake up, and instead of pouring her husband coffee, she would pour for everyone else at the kitchen table. She was mean to him, never poured his coffee, and fed everyone else breakfast. I asked him in private if I could pray that he find a job so we prayed together. After our prayer, he told me that I was a good friend to Isabella.

I accompanied the family for Isabella's baby sister's communion in a Catholic church that was down the street. That day I learned that Isabella's mother, stepfather, and baby sister were attending a Catholic church on Sundays. I thought this was good news and why didn't Isabella tell me. She always expressed how they never wanted to go to church and now they were going so why didn't Isabella tell me that? I smiled and congratulated them. Grateful to attend the communion with the family, I sat admiring her sister who looked like an angel in her all white. Right after the communion, we headed to Isabella's house to gather some food to take to a venue to celebrate with more family and friends. Now her stepfather didn't attend the communion but when we made it to Isabella's house he was in the driveway washing Isabella's mom's car. Her mother was livid and called him all sorts of names. She rushed us all in the car and made him drive in his truck and meet us at the hotel ballroom where they were having the celebration. Her mother said that he was drunk.

I knew that my time would come when I had to stop hanging out with Isabella so much at her house. I would have to withdraw my foot, as the scripture says in, Proverbs 25:17, "Withdraw thy foot from thy neighbor's house; lest he be weary of thee, and so hate thee." Isabella would just call me every day and ask me to come over every weekend and spend the night. Her family had too many issues for me to be in the midst of it all. Isabella was funny though because she would call me to come to eat dinner she cooked for us, but when I got there, she sat at the table not sharing the dinner but on her cell phone, texting a lot. We would go to the living room to watch a movie, and instead of watching it with me, she would be on her cell phone texting. I would tell her that if she wanted to stay on her cell phone, then I could go home. So she would put her cell phone down. She would only put it down for a few minutes and then get right back on it. I could tell something was about to happen between us. I asked Isabella if she and I could pray for our friendship, to which she agreed. I prayed that God would keep us connected and that our friendship would not fall apart. That God would protect our friendship and that nothing would come between us, and that we would stay good friends to each other forever, in Jesus' name. Amen.

I finally asked Isabella who she was texting? She told me that it was a guy named Ludas. He attended their Bible study. I smiled and asked her to show me a picture of him, which she reluctantly did. I needed to see this picture. Once she showed me a picture of him. I told her that he was a wolf in sheep's clothing. She seemed to listen, but I found it strange that when Christmas came around that he bought her a spider head massager. She thought it was a nice gesture for the pain that she was having in her head. I just told her to talk to God about their relationship. I knew in my heart that Isabella would fall hard for this dude. I really hoped that we were not going back down the same road of her not listening as she had done before. I really hoped that she would speak to God about this new romance. I also wondered where the heck was Eric?

Isabella's veterinarian friend who she met in Columbia came to New Jersey to visit, as he stated before. Since Isabella's family lived in a two-family house, the tenant in the second home rented out rooms. I only found out about this when the veterinarian came to visit. He moved upstairs right above Isabella's kitchen. Isabella's stepdad helped him paint his room and even moved the furniture that was in their basement, like a queen-size bed, a big table, TV, and huge dresser. When it was time to eat, they would bang on the ceiling with a broom as a sign that dinner was ready. I shared with Isabella that I wished I had known that her neighbor rented rooms before. I thought maybe I would have moved in, although I was adamant about not renting a room in a stranger's house it was Isabella's neighbor and besides at this time of my life it sounded better than living in my apartment building.

Isabella's stepfather found himself a job in New York. He spent the night a lot in the city so that he didn't have to travel every day from New Jersey, plus he was working long hours. He hired the veterinarian to come and work with him to make some extra money. I would assume that he showed him a good time. I mean Isabella's stepdad liked to party. Now that her stepdad was gone a lot, her mother seemed to miss him and showed her concern. While I believed that he was working hard, since he told us that, I did wonder if he met another woman because he was always gone.

Being Unequally Yoked

While Isabella waited for a job to call her, I asked her to come with me when I did the first video shoot that I was making ministering my poetry. I felt like Isabella could use the break and be inspired to pursue her dreams. I came to pick her up, and the moment I came to her house, her mother stared at me and began to fuss at Isabella for attempting to leave without having a job. This concerned her mother to the point that she argued with her, so Isabella almost didn't leave. I don't know how we left, but we did.

I met Sam the videographer at a local park during one of the events the kids' center hosted for their community. The event was called family day, centered on the health and beauty of the community. I ministered three of my poems on their stage. Families were scattered all over the place, and I thought no one listened, but when I went to get something to eat, one of their vendors said that he liked how I shared my poetry. He asked me a whole bunch of questions. Sam had missed me, as he came in the middle of the day. I watched Sam from behind as he recorded different performances. I approached him and we exchanged contact information. I inquired about his prices and I quickly became impressed that his prices were lower than other videographers. He was within my budget and I knew that I had to work with him sooner than later. I had the vision to have a recording of ministering some of my poems, to be uploaded into iTunes to be distributed on a broader scale, and this would introduce me to a wider audience. I had a plan and was focused on accomplishing this. With the help of Jesus, this shall come to pass.

A week before my recording I had asked one of my banquet managers from where I worked if I could use one of our conference rooms. He said yes and told me that it would not cost me anything. That was awesome because free was also in my budget. I knew that I had to keep this a secret, so I had all of us to enter the building through the back. I couldn't afford anyone noticing me, being jealous and all up in my business. I came prepared with a brand new outfit for my poetry, and another outfit for my praise dance performance. Isabella sat on top of the kitchen counter as she watched me periodically. She would pop her head up a few times from texting to lend some advice, like for me to spit out my gum. When it was all over and done, we were tired and hungry. We took several congratulatory pictures with Sam's professional camera. I felt energized and grateful for this opportunity that God had blessed me with. I paid Sam's assistant the full amount that was due because I had it on me, and I trusted Sam's word that the editing would be complete in one month.

The following weekend I went to pick Isabella up to go to the movies to see Hercules. Isabella was the one that suggested Hercules. We sat down, and I was equally anticipating seeing The Rock's performance. He was not only handsome but he was a fairly decent actor. We had been sitting there for a little when the scenes in the movie were about other gods got me to wanting to get up and walk out of the theater. When it got to the part of how Hercules was born, I had had enough and walked out. Isabella followed behind when she saw that I was not returning. I asked to watch another movie. However, there weren't any other movies that were appropriate for our eyes, so I opted to get my money back. Isabella and I went to get a bite to eat at Applebee's. When we got to her house to tell her brother about the movie and how we walked out. He interrupted me, asking me if I hadn't learned the story of Hercules in high school. Of course, I didn't. I had no idea of its story, but surely Isabella knew and the fact that she knew made me look at her sideways. We definitely were no longer on the same page.

Even though I gave Isabella a hard time for choosing Hercules. I was happy to spend some quality time with her. She was always at Bible study or hanging out with her new friends. She even got really cool with one of the girls who was about her age and who just happened to be engaged to another member of their church. This new friend played an influential role in Isabella's life that when Isabella was in Columbia and barely speaking to me, she was talking to this new girl almost daily. I found that out when Isabella came home and casually told me. I kind of took offense to that because I thought that she didn't call me because she didn't have the time. I surely was wrong. I could tell by the way that Isabella talked about this girl that she wanted to be just like her.

My birthday was around the corner and I wanted Isabella to go with me to a poetry event in a church full of young adults. I was invited by Gloria an acquaintance of mine. Gloria used to be a member of my church but she left and now was attending a different church with lots of youth that host weekly events and one of those events were an open mic that included poets. I could learn a lot and possibly recite some of my poems since they did have an open mic. They were going to have a live DJ, serve food, and it's all on my birthday which made this event sweet. I hoped that Isabella would join me, but one of her church members paid her way to go on an overnight outing that they were having with her church. She said that she would go ahead with me and cancel with her friends. That wasn't necessary since they already paid for her. I would go with Gloria and one of her other lady friends instead.

Outside the church of the poetry event, Gloria, her girl-friend, and I had taken pictures to celebrate the moment. As we entered the church, Gloria and I signed our names on a sheet to be picked to share our poetry on stage. Gloria had been writing poetry and had a piece of paper to read while I walked around the front entrance of the church lobby mem-orizing my poems.

When we entered where the event was being held there were beautiful young hopefuls. I was ecstatic to be sur-rounded by these young adults full of the love of Christ. The DJ was off the chain. I found out his name, DeeJay YNot and he was fantastic. He was playing music that I never heard before. I had to take a picture with him before the event really got started and I had to purchase two of his mix cd that he was selling. I sat down and decided to make myself ready, so I put a black scarf over my face and head. It wrapped around my neck. It's used as a prop and I would take it off at some point of me speaking my poems. I sat there in faith that they would pull my name as they were pulling other names out of the glass jar, but then they called Gloria's name and she went up and did a good job. Moments later I was sweating, just sitting in the front row, waiting for my name to be called, with this black scarf still covering my head and face. I couldn't breathe so I had to take it off. They never called my name anyway.

We went on break and they served us slices of pizza with dessert. When we returned for part two, I had taken that scarf off of my face. Only two more poets were called, with so much time left. The youth began to sing praise songs and pray. They made the announcement that the Holy Spirit had taken over, and they apologized but no more poets would be called at the time. My feelings were crushed. I had been anticipating a turn with a black scarf covering my head and face, just for them to tell us that the Holy Spirit had taken over. I could respect that as we all prayed, speaking in tongues, but I surely wanted a turn. I wished that the Holy Spirit would have waited to come.

When Isabella returned from her weekend trip, I had spent the night at her house to get a recap. We both had a story to tell. I mean, the Lord had taken over at the poetry event and I was still in my feelings, however, I had a blast. I made plans to come back. Isabella said that she enjoyed herself too. It was a memory that she would hold dear to her heart.

A month later, I came over to surprise Isabella with my presence. I walked in through the back door to greet her family, who were in the kitchen. I walked into her bedroom and I jumped because Ludas was sitting on her living room couch. I couldn't believe this girl. Did she not hear me when I was speaking to her about this dude? I walked into her room to see that she was getting ready. She said that her family was invited to a black-tie event, which was why she was getting ready. Immediately I thought about why she didn't invite me. With all the stuff that I had gone through, this would have been a nice treat, and why was this guy going when I told her that he was a wolf in sheep's clothing? I shut the door as we briefly talked. I was disappointed in Isabella's decision, but I didn't let her know. I just gave her a hug. When I walked out of her bedroom towards the kitchen, John had moved from the couch to the kitchen looking suspicious.

I needed a minute to clear my head to figure out what to do concerning my best friend Isabella. My job was my refuge. My job was entertaining in that it was full of life. There was never a dull moment. Denis Rodman walked through the front doors of where I worked. All I could do was act like it didn't faze me. I've never been a fan of his but he was all over the news. To me, Rodman was quiet, polite, and purchased a lot of snacks. I mostly spoke to his representative whenever Rodman came to my establishment. It's interesting that one of my coworkers said that Mr. Rodman asked her about drugs and I heard others say that Mr. Rodman was loud, aggressive, and rude. I didn't see that side of him. I wondered if my coworkers were telling me the truth or just trying to start rumors about an innocent man? I don't know. I just never experienced that side of him.

Once he seemed to get comfortable being around me. He would make small talk. He noticed a black couple sitting down not far from where we were standing. He said to me that he was going over to say hello. When he went over, the first thing that came out of this couple's mouths, was an interrogation of him visiting North Korea. Rodman just walked away. I felt bad for him, like dang, he couldn't even let his guard down without being antagonized. The following weekend when Mr. Rodman came to visit my place of employment with two girls I had never seen before, with an additional man. The ladies separated themselves a few minutes later to come down to purchase some items. While

I rang them up, they were talking to each other, calling Mr. Rodman all kinds of insulting names. I couldn't help but to listen and wonder why these girls were hanging out with him if they didn't like him. Why would they subject themselves to an awful person and then turn around and talk about him like a dog? They could easily have left. Instead, they went back to where Mr. Rodman was. If Mr. Rodman was my friend, I would have told him to stay away from people like that, as if I was his protector. I believe that Mr. Rodman's just needed a spiritual counselor. He looked abused, damaged, and broken. At least that's what I perceived in my spirit.

The night that I met a Hip Hop Magician while at work, He showed me and my boss one of his magic tricks. I actually never seen a coin disappear right in front of my eyes. I wanted to see more. The way that he wore that jogging suit just made me interested in knowing who was this character standing in front of me engaging? He mentioned that he was in BET commercials, so I thought that I remembered him, but I wasn't a follower. He had my attention. We exchanged phone numbers. We talked on the telephone a few times. I looked him up online to find out that he had his own business and that he did magic for little children. I felt like although I was not into magicians, this relationship came across as innocent. On the other hand, with my walk with God, this seemed a little odd.

He said that he was a child of God, and so I dismissed his career. We made plans for him to drive back to New Jersey from New York so that we could have lunch together. It did cross my mind that I was walking a dangerous line but this would be innocent. It's an innocent lunch date. I got to eat. I just convinced myself that this was manageable. But then I went to church that Sunday to hear my pastor preach about not entertaining witchcraft and magicians. I mean, I would have thought my pastor was inside of our conversations. My pastor said so much about this, like not being unequally yoked and witchcraft so much during his sermon, that I felt like God was speaking to me. I knew in my mind that God didn't approve of me hanging out with this nice fella and God had to step in and make it clear. I canceled my date with the Magician. Soon after this, God spoke to me and told me that I was not allowed to date. I didn't know why God said this, but I assumed that He had already told me that He had a man for me and to trust that. Also, I was a sucker for love, and I would fall for a man so quickly and totally dismiss all signs of why I shouldn't be dating that person. I had a lot to lose if I entertained the wrong person again. I came into agreement with Jesus.

At home, my apartment building was already getting on my nerves with the lack of cleanliness. I found myself disgusted every time I walked into the building and embarrassed when I walked out. It didn't use to be this way. I used to be grateful that I had a place to stay. But now so much had changed within me. I had grown a lot and it was time for a major change. I continued to take Bible classes at my church at night on the days I was off from work. One evening I was taking the elevator to my apartment when a tall, young black man with a hole in his throat took the elevator with me, headed to my floor. I didn't say anything to him other than hi, because he spoke first. I didn't know this man, but I recognized him as the same man who used to be on the first floor whenever I would enter my building. Sometimes he would be standing in the entry lobby. A long time ago, while we both were in the elevator, he had a small TV in hand and asked me if I wanted it. I said no.

As I was headed to my apartment, I saw that he was walking into an apartment that was close to mine. Soon after I would leave my apartment at night since I worked the overnight shift, and this tall dude would be leaving his apartment as I passed by, to enter the elevator with me. I didn't say anything to him, not even a hello. At first, he wasn't so obvious, but then I came out of my apartment earlier than usual, and as I was walking in his direction to pass his door, I noticed that he was standing with his door cracked open like he was waiting for me to walk by. When he saw that it was me passing, he rushed out of the door to get on the elevator with me. This concerned me, but I kept my composure. I knew in my heart that this dude was waiting on me and now I was going to have to change the times I left my apartment and start back taking the stairs sometimes, just to throw him off.

This worked for a few weeks, but his twisted mind had him boldly and randomly knock on my door at night time. I looked out my peephole to see him standing outside my door. This man didn't know me and had only seen me in passing, and now he had the nerve to knock on my door. I gave him no reason to harass me. This was beyond disturbing. I didn't answer his knock, and the following night when he knocked on my door again, I called the police. The police officer told me since I never said anything to this man to cause this kind of behavior, for me to not say a word to him. The police officer said that if this guy did anything to me, for me to call them immediately.

I walked out of my apartment building, talking to my mother on the phone. When I hung up, I happened to look across the street to see this man turned around to the opposite side of the street, with a black hoodie on like he was trying to be unrecognizable. I had a made up mind that this guy was crazy. I wondered, how he knew the times that I was walking out of my apartment. Even when I started to take the stairs, he would be outside at the right time or stand by the elevator. This was strange to me.

Then the Lord led me to look out my window while it was pitch black inside my apartment. I looked out my window and just diagonally from my window, I could see my neighbor's window. Sure enough, this tall black man with a hole in his neck was standing at the window with his lights on, looking in my direction. Then I figured out that he knew the time that I was getting up to get ready for work, because I turned on the light, and each time I turned off the light was a signal that I was walking out my door. I changed my routine immediately by getting dressed in the dark, even doing my hair and makeup. I walked out the door at odd times. This worked because I didn't see this jerk. However, I did come to work looking a hot mess. I would have to adjust myself every night I arrived at work.

When I was much younger, not walking with God, if someone told me that some guy was following them for no reason, I would not have believed them. I always used to think that a woman gave a man a reason, but now that I was experiencing it, I knew for a fact that it was possible to not even know the person's name, and they will still harass and stalk you. I continued to pray for protection and I began not to see this guy.

I reported this to the maintenance man, but he seemed not to believe me. Plus I think that he was upset with me since I complained about his team not doing their work. The maintenance man got worse with his behavior. I would see him out and about in the town when he should have been in our building, making sure the building was secure and clean. A lot of people were getting on my nerves. I just knew that God had something better for me. I had been patient, but a change would have to come soon.

I had issues with my car where it kept stopping on me and my mechanic would fix it and then the problem would reoccur. This happened ongoing, which caused me to be even more behind on rent. I was already a month behind from when I took over the lease, plus I was late on my rent every month. Now I was going to be not one but two months behind because I had to get my car fixed. I tried to talk with the apartment management company to explain my dilemma. They had always been understanding and they seemed to be willing to work with me, but I was too behind. I received an eviction notice for non-payment of rent. I couldn't believe that this was happening to me yet again. Another eviction that I would have to experience. I mean, when I really thought about it, I was eagerly waiting for an exit from my apartment building. However, I didn't want it to come in this way of eviction.

While visiting Isabella at her home, I learned that their visitor who came from Columbia was moving back to Columbia. I knew this was my opportunity to inquire about the room. If I could rent that room when he moved out. Isabella already told me what their friend was paying in rent which was half the price that I was paying at my apartment. To live right above my best friend was a no brainer and I could afford the rent. Isabella set up a meeting with her neighbor Linda who was renting out the room. Isabella and her family knew that I had to move out of my please soon so they quickly reached out to Linda on my behalf.

The day had come for me to meet Linda so I went upstairs to the second home adjacent to Isabella's. Linda was soft-spoken and walked me to the room that I would be renting. All of the furniture that Isabella and her family gave the young guy was all in there. She took me on a tour of the house and told me that I was welcome to sit in her living room and use their kitchen. She told me that the rent was half the price that I was paying at the apartment. Even though this was smaller with a shared bathroom with two other men. Linda told me the other two roommates, who were Hispanic men, were at work and all was quiet in their room. She said that I would probably not see them since they worked during the day and I worked overnight. We shook hands to seal the deal and I walked back down to Isabella's house, feeling relieved that I had a place to live when I moved out of the apartment. However, I did have questions for Isabella since she didn't mention the other roommates were men. Good thing God kept Isabella from spilling that tea otherwise I would have not considered moving in there.

I had a couple of days to move out before the sheriff was to come and lock me out. I decided to only pack some of my clothes, shoes, and bags, and bring some of my personal items, like papers and journals with me to my room inside Linda's house. I left all of my furniture and decorative stuff right there in that apartment. I refused to bring any bugs to this new place. I needed a fresh new start.

The guy whose room I was taking over only had a couple of days to stay in New Jersey before moving back to Columbia. I asked if I could go ahead and move into the room which he was fine with. He stayed in Isabella's house for his last couple of days. Isabella's mother offered for me to keep the furniture in the room, which made sense in saving money but I had my own plans. The items in the room were too big and bulky. I wanted a desk and the room didn't have a closet so I would have to purchase a portable closet. Isabella's step-father and a friend came to remove the items from the room and I slept a few nights on an air mattress. It didn't take long for the Holy Spirit to lead me in the direction of purchasing my own furniture. I was driving to East Orange to get a bag of hair when I noticed a sign outside of this store across the street from the traffic light that showed household goods. I turned the corner and parked in the parking lot of CVS that was across the street from this furniture place. I entered this small business that seemed small on the outside, but once I went inside it was pretty big. They not only sold household goods but furniture too. I purchased a twin-size bed with a desk and headboard. My room didn't have a closet, so I purchased a free-standing closet, which worked out perfectly. I made two different purchases, which totaled less than $500, including delivery. Talk about blessings. I didn't have to sleep on the floor for too long, which my spirit was not at ease about. I didn't know why, but after that first night, I got an uncomfortable feeling.

I walked the streets with confidence, doing my laundry at the laundromat. I took a break to walk to the local dollar store to get a snack when I ran into one of my old neighbors from the apartment building. I shared with her why I no longer lived there and about my stalker. I described this stalker to her, and she knew exactly who I was talking about. She told me that the police kicked him out of the building. He was no longer allowed to step foot in that apartment building because the tenants were complaining about him. He was robbing the Latino men. He would stand in the building, waiting for them to come in and out, and he would take their money. I knew that guy was crazy and it wasn't just me. If the maintenance man had listened to me, this would not have happened. God saved me again, Psalm 34:8, "O taste and see that the LORD is good: blessed is the man that trusteth in him."

CHAPTER TEN

Prayer

I liked the idea of living right upstairs from Isabella and her family. We had plans that every time that her family cooked when they finished cooking they would bang on the ceiling for me to come down to eat as they did for their friend who came to visit. The weirdest thing happened between Isabella and me. She didn't knock on the ceiling when the food was ready. As a matter of fact, I watched Ludas come in and out of her house. She completely chose Ludas over me. I wanted her to come and look at my new room but she decided not to come through. She obviously did not listen to me when I said this dude was a wolf in sheep's clothing, or she just didn't care. I mean he looked the part of a gentleman and churchgoer, but I could discern that he was not. I also saw it when he walked in front of me, carrying a toolbox to Isabella's house. It was his back that gave me confirmation that this dude was not the man he presented himself to be, to Isabella and to her family. I could discern not only in the picture but now through his body.

Isabella and I had been friends for five years. We had traveled this road of being churchgoers, celibate, Christian women who were all about God, but now I could tell that by her hanging out with this wolf in sheep's clothing things were about to change. Although Isabella saw herself finding a godly man, the reality was that she didn't. Unfortunately, Satan hadn't shown her his intent. To me, it was rather odd that God would bring a man to her just when she came back from her Columbia trip, knowing that she had a lot of insecurities. Isabella seemed to have decided to do whatever she felt like doing, therefore, I held my tongue to be careful about what I had to say because I've learned that there's power in my tongue and what I bless on earth God blesses and what I curse heaven curses.

Ludas went from picking up Isabella for church on Sunday to coming over her house every weekend. Although I was furious with Isabella and we seemed to be going in opposite directions, I still found myself not knowing how to separate myself from her family. They had been so good to me that I didn't feel like I could disconnect myself from them.

I was at home, being bored over the weekend. Isabella wasn't at her house because Ludas car wasn't there, so I went to her house to say hello to her parents. Her mother was in her bedroom, doing laundry. While we talked, I helped her fold laundry. Then Isabella and Ludas returned to her home. Isabella came to her mother's bedroom. She must've heard my voice, so she stood around for a second and then went back to the kitchen with Ludas. I felt weird being in her home and not talking to her like our usual selves, so I left. On my way out the door, Isabella was at the refrigerator, handing Ludas pasta, asking him what type he wanted to eat.

Isabella became quickly involved with Ludas so that she not only dismissed me but her little sister. Isabella was out most weekends with Ludas, leaving her baby sister alone. I would see her sister playing in the front yard by herself. I felt bad for her, so with her mother's permission, I took her to this new yogurt place in town. The following week, I took her baby sister with me as I got my car washed. My car air conditioner would not work, so we were hot, and the car stopped on us and barely turned back on. This was humiliating, but also a sign that maybe I should slow down and not hang out with her baby sister so much. I was thinking that this was not my responsibility or place. Isabella heard about our time together, because she started to take her sister on outings. I thought that it was funny when I saw Isabella and Ludas come back with her baby sister from the local fair, with one side of their faces covered up in face paint.

Isabella wanted so bad to be in a relationship with a man that they were willing to put on an incredible show. Ludas, for me, was a pretender. Satan is one deceitful and crafty monster. He would go to extreme measures to make us believe that he was the real deal when he was a counterfeit.

I had this strong desire to stand on my porch every night to watch Isabella walk by with Ludas in hopes that she would be reminded of the woman of God that she is. After my evening class, I went to grab a bite to eat, so by the time I got home, it was close to midnight. I looked up to spot Isabella and Ludas leaving her house. I hurried up to my room to my bed in disbelief and upset with Isabella. I called her cell phone to leave her an outraged voice message, asking her why was she leaving her house so late and where was she going with him. I was highly disappointed in her actions, the fact that she allowed him to take her out of the house at that time of night dang near morning. To me, this was just the beginning. I knew that I had to try again to talk some sense into her. I desperately needed her to see what I was saying about Ludas being a wolf in sheep's clothing and this was not a joke. This wolf was taking her down a road of immorality, and it was only a matter of time.

After the weekend, I knew that it was my opportunity to talk to Isabella and knock some sense into her. Ludas car was not outside, so I called Isabella to ask her if I could come down to talk to her briefly, and to my amazement, she agreed. She was doing laundry in her basement when I arrived. We sat across from each other and I shared my thoughts and concerns with her. I reminded her of me calling Ludas a wolf in sheep's clothing. I told her that it was not a good idea for her to leave her house so late with this guy and that if he was the man of God that she said he was, then he would have her out at a respectable time. She responded by telling me that she and Ludas realized that they should not have done that and they prayed about it together. She also mumbled that she broke off their relationship once before. As if to say that I was not about to persuade her into ending their relationship again.

Isabella stopped talking and I picked the conversation back up, but her stare and smirk let me know that she didn't take me seriously and it was a waste of my time to keep talking. I could discern by her look that she thought that I was also being jealous. I shut that down by telling her that I was not jealous of her and that I knew that other people were telling her that but it was the farthest from the truth. She didn't say a word as she looked at me stunned that I knew and my comment also made her smirk disappear. I reminded her that this was the third time that I had to go through this with her concerning men. I decided to change the subject but before I laid this topic to rest I ended it by telling her that she was the one who had to live with her decisions at the end of the day. I really wanted her to understand where I was coming from and that it was coming from a loving place. We began to talk about her new job and coworkers. I was happy for Isabella in that she found a new job that she really liked. I missed her and only hoped that she would change her mind and actions regarding Ludas so that we could continue on this road of friendship.

It was a good thing that we switched the topic, as her brother came creeping down the stairs, probably wondering what we were talking about. He hated that I always had something negative to say about Isabella's boyfriend choices. Her brother condoned sin. He supported bad behavior. I mean this was a guy who lived in his room day and night, who wouldn't get a job, and smoked weed and other drugs that had his bedroom reeking.

Often times I saw Isabella walking past with Ludas, and she never spoke to me. She didn't look over at me when I was standing on the porch. Oh, but when she was with her family and Ludas was not there, she waved, smiled, and spoke to me. Her ignoring me at times really hurt my feelings.

The truth of the matter was that we were friends. I mean God called this girl my best friend and we lived close to each other. So when I saw her, I spoke, even when she was with Ludas. I never spoke to him.

Ludas went from picking Isabella up for church on Sunday to spending the night at her house over the weekend. In my mind, Isabella may have believed this was harmless fun. She entered the world of temptation. Honestly, I couldn't believe Isabella. We were just talking in her basement and now he was spending the night. This girl was stressing me out. I grew grey hair underneath my wig. Why did I have to live right above her to see it all?

It also seemed that this dude was working overtime to prove that he was harmless and not this wolf in sheep's clothing. I could tell that Isabella told him what I said. When he came to visit her, he would always walk the opposite side of the street like a little coward. He also got a newer car. When they started dating, he was driving a nice little white station wagon-looking car, and then he switched it to a brand new Honda. I believe that Ludas was desperately trying to impress Isabella and her family with a new car because of the lifestyle that they lived. He purchased it because he was manipulating himself to maneuver into their lives. I could recognize Satan's devices a mile away. Ludas had Isabella wrapped around his finger in the most cunning way possible. There was no way that I had this strong discernment if it was not of God. I hoped that God used others to tell her the truth. I mean from my experience usually Jesus uses many people and situations to grab your attention but it's up to us to pay attention and be obedient to change. I wondered what the heck was she learning at her church that she attended every Sunday with Ludas? Was she even listening to her preacher because I knew that God had to use him to deliver a message from the pulpit? I wondered if her Bible study buddies knew that Ludas was spending the night over her house? It ran through my mind to call her church and tell on her.

At home I had deal with my own issues. When I moved into my room, there was one issue that I had that the landlord brought to my attention. She mentioned that the toilet did not flush properly sometimes. She pointed to me a bowl that was sitting on top of the refrigerator that was placed in the hall for the tenants to share. She said to fill this bowl with water and this would help flush. I looked at her like she must be crazy. I would never do that. The other issue that I saw after the toilet, not flushing was that the shower head had mold on it which was disgusting to look at. To shower with that shower head freaked me out. I knew that I had to do something soon about getting them fixed. I sent a text to the landlord about these two issues. She said that she contacted the owner but he hadn't responded to her. To me, that was strange, since the owners lived in a house right next door to us. The landlord made it seem that the owners were ignoring her and they never come up to fix anything. That was not the impression that I got from them. I knew them before I became a tenant and they were always friendly and helpful. Shoot, the owner even tried to fix my car on two occasions. I found it hard to believe that they didn't care to maintain the keep up of their house that they owned.

The last straw that I had with this toilet issue was when I was running late for work, due to plunging the toilet. Not to mention the numerous times I walked in the bathroom to see the tenants leaving their poop in the toilet for someone else to flush. I had enough, so I stayed awake and waited to hear the owners arrive home from work. Once I heard the owner's truck, I ran outside to ask him to fix these two issues. I already went to Walmart to purchase a new shower head and one of the male tenants tried to replace it for me, but whatever he was trying to do it didn't work. As soon as I told the owner these issues, he sent two of his male workers upstairs with their tools and the situation got handled. I figured that the landlord didn't put in the effort as I did which confused me. Either way, I sent her a text that this matter got handled and the owner indeed fixed the problem. I could see Isabella and Ludas with her parents in the kitchen as I thanked the owner for coming so fast to make the repairs.

Some time had passed and I don't know what made Isabella decide to come to my church. I had just arrived and parked when Isabella and Ludas parked right in front of me. I sat in my car, looking at them with a surprised look on my face. I could hear Isabella say to Ludas as they got out of his car, "There's Diana." He just looked away and she walked in with him. I just observed, but I wondered what were they doing there? Maybe God had a word for her and maybe this time she would listen. I sat down in church, and then there came Isabella to sit in my section, just a row in front of me. Like why would she sit so close to me? I just got up to when the praise music came on and I praised and worshipped the Lord. When it was time for us to sit down, I went to grab my stuff and sat in another section of the church. I was not about to be uncomfortable in my own church due to Isabella's shenanigans.

The pastor began to preach about soul ties with the wrong people. He said that if you are walking with God and have a covenant with someone who is not truly walking with God, either the believer will influence the unbeliever or the unbeliever will influence the believer, and usually, it's the unbeliever that will influence the believer. I knew in my heart that the pastor was specifically talking about Isabella and Ludas. He said in his sermon that God will bless you with new friends, and I felt like God was using my pastor to deliver that message to me. I tell you the truth that nothing got through to Isabella. It just seemed to get worse. Ludas went from spending the night over the weekend to every night. When I would leave home for work at night his car was parked in their driveway and when I returned home Isabella and Ludas would be leaving the front porch with their work clothes on.

I tried to keep myself engrossed with work and the ministry that God had planted inside of me, although it was terribly difficult for me to focus all the way. Isabella stayed on my mind. She was my best friend and I desperately didn't want her to go down the wrong path that she was already on. We were connected spiritually and it hurt me that much more. We went from spending a lot of time together to not even speaking and this hurt my heart.

For Thanksgiving, I had absolutely no plans. In the past, I spent these holidays with either Isabella or Pretty Eyes, but Pretty Eyes was out of town and Isabella, well she was downstairs with her family being happy in love with Satan's son Ludas. Before I headed off to work, I could hear them all downstairs having a good time. Isabella's mother posted quite a few pictures on Facebook of what seemed to be Ludas family in town. They surely looked cute as a couple, taking family photos around the table when Ludas was holding the knife to cut the turkey. The picture of Isabella and Ludas holding each other reminded me of a Lifetime movie.

For Christmas, the food pantry where I volunteered for the past two years was having lunch for their volunteers. I felt really blessed to be fortunate to give back to the needy, especially since I was the person in need not that long ago. I knew that giving back was a part of my journey and should be for everyone who walked on this earth.

The day of Christmas, I had taken a vacation for a week from my job. Instead of staying home to hear the foolery going on beneath me, also I didn't want them to know that I was spending this holiday alone for the day. I stayed in a hotel about forty-five minutes away from my home. I sat in my hotel room over the holiday weekend, ordering room service, going downstairs to make friends with the night auditor, who made me a cup of hot chocolate as we talked near their lobby fireplace. This was just what God ordered for me. Time away to keep me in peace and harmony with the Holy Spirit. God knew this was a hard time for me and He was there to protect me from losing my mind.

Severing Our Friendship

I was over the moon when Pretty Eyes came back to New Jersey to live. She instructed me to go outside, that her sister had something to give me. When I got outside, walking towards her sister's car, Pretty Eyes jumped out. I was pleasantly surprised and opened my arms to give my friend the warmest hug. I took her upstairs to show her my room and I packed a bag to head out to spend the night at her sister's house for the weekend. They were also heading to go to a bar in New York to watch the game. My favorite team was playing, the New England Patriots. I had been a fan ever since the year that they won every game but lost the Super bowl to the Giants. I was still impressed with their winning streak. I felt like they ate some humble pie and was going to win this Super bowl with the help of my prayer. And just like that my prayers were answered and my favorite team won the Super bowl while I hung out with Pretty Eyes and her sister. Now, this was a night to remember. After the game, the bar was turning into a night club well that was our cue to head out. Pretty Eyes and her sister wanted to stay a little longer but that was not the place for me as I already made a promise to myself and God that I wouldn't entertain a night club. So I walked downstairs from where we were sitting and sat my behind by the exit door waiting on Pretty Eyes and her sister. A few minutes came and I heard them telling me to come on. I thought that Pretty Eyes wouldn't want to be in a place like that not even to chill especially since she was going around calling herself a Prophet or something like that.

At Pretty Eyes sister house, she told me that God wanted her to start a ministry, therefore, she wouldn't get a job instead pursue ministry full time. I listened to her intensely, glad to have my girlfriend back in town but I grew concerned for her well-being. We talked until we fell asleep. We slept on opposite sides of the couch. Her sister had one of those long couches that could sit twenty-five people at the same time. The next morning we woke up to a massive amount of snow on the ground.

I decided to wait a little longer to leave in hopes that when the sun comes out it will make the snow soft to make it easier for me to scrap the snow off my car. I also wanted to have a heart-to-heart talk with Pretty Eyes. I started the conversation by saying that this would be the last time that I said this to her, but I believed that it needed to be said. I told her that it was not good for her to not work. I quoted the scripture, 2 Thessalonians 3:10&11, "For even when we were with you, we gave you this rule: If a man will not work, he shall not eat. We hear that some among you are idle. They are not busy, they are busybodies." I even got emotional where tears were falling from my eyes. I told her that I didn't want to see her back to being homeless with no money to live and food to eat. Her sister chimed in and said that we all loved her, but if she did not have plans to work that she could not stay in her apartment, because she needed help taking care of her bills. Pretty Eyes seemed uninterested in what we were saying but I let her know that it was coming from a genuine loving place and I only wanted the best for her. That she could work a normal job while she pursued her dreams. I hugged her and headed to my car as the snow had gotten soft making it manageable for me to drive home.

I checked my email to see that I received an email from Pretty Eyes. She was severing our friendship. She said that God told her to do so. I wished that she would have called me instead of sending me an email. But hey, if she said that God told her, then I had to respect that. This was what I told her in my email response. Pretty Eyes and I had been friends for the same amount of time as Isabella and I. Now I thought maybe I should have kept my mouth shut because I kept losing all of my good friends. I know that God didn't call me to be quiet.

At my church, they were about to hold a ceremony for all of their graduates. I was one of the students to receive a certificate in biblical studies while the other students were receiving a much higher degree. I needed to tell somebody, so when I saw Isabella outside of my house when she was in her truck with her sister I blurted out that I was having a graduation ceremony at the church the coming Sunday. Isabella smiled and said congratulations. I was hoping that she would show up despite what we had been going through. I was still her friend. On Sunday my church didn't disappoint. They had a room for the students to put on their caps and gowns. Most of the students had their families or friends in attendance while I had no one. Not even Isabella showed up when I needed her to. As much as this was a letdown I didn't allow this disappointment to steal my joy from accomplishing a milestone. When my pastor called my name and introduced me as a poet I was amused and happily accepted my certificate.

I was driving from church when I saw Pretty Eyes walking. I looked her way which she put her hands over her face and turned her head as if she was trying to disguise herself. Wow, I thought to myself. We bumped into each other another day, and for some reason, she was receptive to me picking her up. I was open to continuing our friendship. I wasn't the one who ended it. I picked her up at a house where she was staying and we went to get a bite to eat. She told me that God told her to move back to our town. She was staying at a friend's house before they sold it. Her friend's mother passed away, so she lived there along with her friend's two brothers, who made it very clear that she was not welcome to stay there. The house was on the grounds of a graveyard. I thought that was creepy, but hey, if God led her there then He would protect her there. I felt the need to take care of Pretty Eyes and make sure that she was okay.

Every other day I picked her up and gave her a couple of dollars. I asked her how she was eating on the days that I didn't see her. She told me that she was eating food at a church that just started to cook food for the needy. They cooked fish and steak meals. After speaking with Pretty Eyes I was at ease knowing that she was eating good.

We sat in the park, talking about our hopes and dreams. She had big ones along with me. I was heading to New York to record a song I wrote at night. It was a gospel song and I found this recording studio, as they advertised on a gospel radio station. They had a package of $1500 to record, which included placing the song on iTunes, YouTube, and so many other places where they released music. I found this to be a great opportunity, but I asked the producer if I could pay less if I didn't include the website that they offered and if I would take my own photos for the cover. So the producer agreed and I didn't have to pay the $1500. It was less. I asked Pretty Eyes if she could take my pictures, which she agreed to do. I picked her up and we went to a place that had a lot of green grass and a brick wall. I wore a bright blue jumpsuit with cream shoes, purchased a new wig and did my own makeup. She took my pictures like a professional photographer using her iPhone. Following the photo shoot, we headed to a local restaurant that I wanted to introduce to her. The food was slamming. They gave us enough food that we shared. While eating I knew in my heart that Pretty Eyes and I were going to separate. I knew that this was going to be the final time that we would be together as friends. I gave her some money and I dropped her off at her house. Pretty Eyes went her way and I went mine.

I sat at my favorite café, typing my third book when I looked up. Pretty Eyes was about to enter, but when she saw me she didn't open the door but took her hands off the door and walked up the hill. I sent her an email that it was not necessary for her to walk away whenever she saw me. We would cross paths since we lived in the same town. It was not good for us to act like enemies. I wrote in that email that when we saw each other we could speak and that I was okay with us not continuing our friendship. She never responded to my email which I didn't expect her to. I just hoped that she did read it and know that I was cool with her. I saw her again at that same cafe a few weeks later. I was entering as she was sitting, working on her laptop. I ordered my food to go but while I waited I was walking in her direction to speak, but she gave me the notion like "don't come close." I got the food that I ordered and walked out the door without saying a word to Pretty Eyes. I loved Pretty Eyes and while she was acting as if we were strangers I still wanted nothing but the best for her.

I needed a break, and wouldn't you know that God gave me just that. One of the young ladies from my church who I helped complete a special project wanted to treat me to a day in New York. I don't get to go to New York that often. It's a special treat whenever I go and I still consider myself to be that of a tourist. We had planned for me to drive to her house and she would park her car at the mall to ride the bus into New York early morning so that we would spend the entire day in New York. The morning that we were going to New York, my car got towed. I had my car parked on the street during the times the signs said to not park because of the town would be cleaning the streets. I thought that I would wake up in enough time to move my car, but I over-slept and woke up with no car in front of my home. One of the policemen directed me to where my car had been towed. I convinced the owner of the shop where my car was parked to give me the keys to my car with the promise that I would pay him on my next paycheck. He believed me and handed me the keys to my car and allowed me to drive my car off of his lot. I really appreciated God for giving me grace. I only had enough money for New York City and nothing else. I thanked God that I didn't have to cancel our trip.

I drove my car to meet my friend and she drove us to the bus we would take into New York. I was like a kid looking forward to a field trip. She had no idea what this trip meant to me. I was cute too. I wore this short-sleeve grey shirt that had a huge cross on the front of it that was covered in many different colors and rhinestones. I wore ripped jeans and the back of my shirt was longer than the front. Our first stop was visiting a museum that was three floors. I had my girlfriend take lots of pictures of me while she took none for herself. They also had a roof where they served you food and you could either sit where there were chairs or on the section where they had fake grass. It was awesome. We sat there after about three hours of touring this museum, which was educational.

When we were done, we walked toward Central Park, and on our way, I noticed a face that was familiar. It was the man who used to live in the shelter with me, who went to church with me every Sunday. He was working outside with the Salvation Army. We greeted each other and I asked him how he was doing. He smiled and told me that he was doing great. I smiled, gave him a genuine hug, and kept walking. That was strange to bump into him. With all the people who lived in New York, I bumped into him. There was a food truck nearby where I saw a young lady order some kind of chicken burrito that looked spicy, and something that I couldn't pass up, so I ordered one too. It was rather huge. My friend didn't eat, but I did. We walked to Central Park to sit for a little bit so that we could take a break and I could enjoy the burrito. We sat comfortably, looking towards a small lake. Where we sat there were a few people spread about, even people on both sides of us. As we sat there just enjoying the sun, winding down, I heard two men ask us if we could take a picture of them. I turned their way and excitedly said of course. I was the queen of taking people's pictures. One man handed me his camera and I stood up all smiles. Both men were eye candy. As I was positioning myself to take their picture, one of the men said that their marriage was tomorrow. I took the camera away from my face before I could snap their picture and I told them that I did not support that. I apologized to them and handed their camera back to them. They said okay and took their camera back and walked away, looking sad. I thought that was odd that they picked my friend and me out of all the people in the park to want us to take their picture. Here I was this churchgoer with this huge cross on my shirt and of all people I was chosen. That was interesting. When I sat down, a man who looked like he was from Africa was sitting to the right of us said that these two men had been in the park for a while, trying to find someone to take their picture.

My friend and I sat there at the park for a little while longer before we continued our walk. There were some local performances that we stayed around to listen to. It was all nice. I went home feeling loved by Jesus. I forgot all about my pain. I must say that I did get paid and I went back to that owner of the towing company and I gave him every penny of the money I owed him. He thanked me and told me that he knew that I was coming back.

My birthday was coming up, so I decided to take myself horseback riding and out to eat. Olivia invited me to come to Florida and said she was going to take me to Disney World. Now, this was a place that I mentioned that I wanted to go when I had my online interview, and now this blessing was upon me. I felt like it was time for me to be present for my distant family and friends and put in that effort.

My first night in Florida, she and I took pictures in her house before we stepped out to a comedy club. I laughed from the moment we stepped in the door, all the way until we left. I must say there was one comedian who was not funny and the audience lets him know it by not laughing at his jokes. The host quickly came in and intervened and he was more hilarious. This was just what my body and mind needed. The next day Olivia had dropped me off at the beach while she headed to work. I was in the sun all day prepared. I had my cell phone for music, soaked up the sun and ran in and out of the pool. For about five hours it seemed that I had the beach all to myself and then people started coming towards the time that I was leaving. I sat and had lunch on their boardwalk eating pasta. The next day after this Olivia and I headed to Orlando to go to Disney, and we stayed at a hotel where I could get us a discount. I ran out of money but I was getting paid again in a few days, so I asked Olivia to pay for my food with the intentions of me paying her back before

I left Florida. Why did I have to ask her for that? She gave me the nastiest attitude the entire time we were at Disney. I tried hard to not let her attitude bother me. She was irritated with me. She didn't even want to take my picture when I posed with Mickey Mouse and she went missing when I was ready to take pictures with some of the other characters. In the end, we did have a good time. I liked seeing the parade. Towards the end of the show, we sat down on the grass with hundreds of people to watch the final display of fireworks that were going off above the castle. We drove to the hotel in good spirits and the next morning we drove back to her home which was about a four-hour ride. By the time we got to her house, I had fever blisters all over my mouth.

I spent three days cooped up in the room until my final day. Olivia got me to go with her to Miami to walk the board-walk and indulge in a meal. I still had fever blisters but they weren't that visible in the night time which is when we walked the Miami streets. My friend thought that she was slick by saying that she had to use the restroom inside of the club. This would be the only way that she could get me to go inside of anybody's club. Some men followed us there too attempting to talk to me, but I ignored them. I waited for Olivia at the door.

Thank Jesus for fulfilling a dream of mine. I had a good time in Florida but it was time to go back to New Jersey to focus on the ministry. I was having the worst kind of experiences with producers of music and video. The videographer never supplied me with the video that he was supposed to be working on. Every week there was a different excuse as to why the video wasn't ready. I had to threaten to send him to court after I had already paid him in full. He apologized a million times as to why the video never rendered. Subsequently, I had to count it as a loss. I never received the entire video and he made it clear that I would not receive the video in its entirety. I did learn two lessons, one to never pay anyone that is doing work for me in full upfront also to sign a contract. Pay them after the job is done and to my satisfaction.

The recording producer who was going to record my first gospel record in New York basically fed me a lot of promises where he couldn't produce. The day of the recording I had taken a cab into New York City. This cab driver waited for me for four hours until I was done recording my music to take me back to New Jersey. When I received the final version of my song by email it was nothing like what I recorded and I didn't recognize any of the instruments. He remixed it so bad with auto tunes that I didn't recognize my own voice. You would think that I was this horrible singer that needed auto tunes. In my disappointment and grief, I went ahead and paid this recording producer the rest of the money. But it sucked that I worked hard, signed a contract, and paid in full just to be distressed.

Reprobate Mind

Ludas seemed to have broken up with Isabella and her family. I didn't see his car parked outside her house nor did I see him coming around. I saw Isabella and I tell you the truth I wasn't mad about his disappearance. I would think that Isabella and Ludas were getting married the way they carried on. I have some ideas of what I think transpired, either Isabella's mom got tired of Ludas being at her house every single night for nine months or Isabella's brother got into an argument that escalated to Ludas having to leave the house. Either way, I was happy not to see him parked outside her house at night and coming out of the house early morning. A few months later I was coming home in the morning after a long night at work when Isabella apparently was coming home too with an overnight bag. She tried to hold the bag behind her when she saw me but it was too late I had already seen it.

Then I was at church on a Friday night for Holy Ghost night. We worshipped God all night with song and dance. We had so much fun worshipping God in spirit and in truth. By the time we left the church, it was close to eleven o'clock. I drove home just filled with the Holy Spirit. I parked across the street from my home, since there was no parking in front. Isabella and Ludas were sitting in the car. I walked past them while looking in their direction which both of them looked down to not make eye contact with me. I felt in my spirit that Isabella had fornicated with Ludas for the first time. She did what we promised not to do. Up until that point I never felt like they were intimate with each other sexually. It just never seems like they crossed the line of fornication but this night seemed to have been the night. I mean Isabella looked down as if to give the impression that she was ashamed and oh Ludas just had his head down for no other reason than to confirm the name that I called him from day one.

It was inevitable if she's going to be spending the night over a grown man's house. I don't care how many church services they attend together. You are bound to fall into temptation. A week following this episode I came home in the evening when it was pouring down rain. For some reason, I didn't get out of my car. I looked up to see that Isabella was moving out of her mom's house. Her truck was parked two cars behind me. She came out of the house with a frantic look on her face as she passed me with Ludas. When they made it to her truck I could see in my rearview mirror that she and Ludas were talking in the rain. She drove her truck up to the back of her house, and just like that my friend moved out of her house to move in with Ludas. At first, I kept blaming Ludas for the person she had become, but then I had to realize that it was Isabella too. She knew the dangers. She was a willing participant.

To see my once best friend move out to play house caused me great sorrow. I would go on Facebook to see Isabella's mother posting pictures of Isabella and Ludas at parties that Isabella once talked badly about. Ludas was with alcohol in his hand and she was staring into his eyes. Then there was a picture that seemed like Isabella's mother posted to taunt me because she knew that I was watching. I decided since Isabella moved out that I didn't feel the need to be reminded of her actions, therefore, I unfriended her mother. I wondered when Isabella looked in the mirror at herself what did she see? Did she have any convictions? Did she miss our friendship and the road that we traveled together? God gave me this scripture in the time of my hurt, confusion, and concern about Isabella's walk. 1 John 2:19, "They went out from us, but they were not of us: for if they had been of us, they would no doubt have continued with us: but they went out, that they might be made manifest that they were not all of us." God gave me another scripture, Romans 1:28-32.

I asked Isabella's stepmother for her new phone number since she changed it. I desperately needed her to see this message while she was ignoring signs and walked this earth like everything was Gucci. I sent a group text of the Romans 1:28-32 scripture along with an in-depth message about having a reprobate mind. I didn't mention any names but by Isabella's response of rebuking me, I felt like she knew that this message was directed at her.

It was necessary that I let Isabella go. If I saw her, I wasn't going to speak. I didn't feel the pressure to save face for her family. Her family no longer cared for me nor did Isabella, shoot she didn't even speak. They collectively dismissed me and chose the wolf in sheep's clothing over me. It was time for me to celebrate some milestones happening in my life. I was about to celebrate five years working at my job, which was a major accomplishment for a girl who in the past couldn't hold down a job longer than a year, 1 Corinthians 2:9, "But as it is written, Eye hath not seen, nor ear heard, neither have entered into the heart of man, the things which God hath prepared for them that love him."

At work, I met a pastor who stood in front of me from Illinois, where I once lived. He pastored a church that I attended while staying in Illinois. I knew that I had to see if he would be willing to give me advice. He had flown around the world, even to Africa. He was married, with a newborn, and a best-selling author. A megachurch in New Jersey flew him out to see if he could lend a hand in the creative department. I asked him if one day he could talk to me and give me some advice on how he had been able to be successful. He said that we could talk about it over lunch. We made plans to meet at a local diner near the job during the day.

After my shift, I went home got some rest, then jumped up four hours later to get showered and dressed to meet this pastor at the local diner. He was there sitting down, waiting on me. We had a pleasant conversation. He talked more about his newborn child and wife. I was happy for him, but he didn't give me much advice other than to wait and be still. While he talked and I listed, he said that I had a lash by my eye. He leaned over and with his fingers he gently removed the lash off of my face. For two seconds I froze, not knowing how to react to that. I never had a man put his hand on my face so gently. I mean usually, someone is telling me that I have something on my face so that I can remove it.

I walked towards my car when our meeting was over, that's when he asked me to come with him to see his rental car. He said that he wanted to show me what was cool about his car. I reluctantly agreed to follow him, but when I got in his car there was not anything spectacular. My job hosted car shows so I wasn't impressed. I just knew in my heart that I had to get out of his presence. As he leaned towards me, I excused myself with a smile and headed to my car. I couldn't believe that he was making moves on me. This big-time Christian man with a newborn baby who was a best-selling author.

All I wanted to do was go home and get far away from him. We became Facebook friends, and all I wanted to do was correct his behavior by sending him a private message, but God stopped me. I sensed that God did not want me to be that person to put this pastor in his place. God would take care of this matter and any other hidden offenses. I just left that entire situation alone and put that in God's hand.

At work one of the members of the Beach Boys came to talk to me. I could tell that he had been slightly intoxicated. He asked me questions that I answered. I told him that I wanted to be a singer. He recommended a book for me to read, titled, "All You Need To Know About The Music Business." I immediately went to Barnes and Noble and picked that book up. I read this book in its entirety. The best advice that a girl like me could receive. You see, the pastor couldn't help me, but God sent one of the Beach Boys to do what the pastor wouldn't.

I met new celebrities at my job like new bosses. My final overnight Manager, Ben, was an older man who had diabetes. He had a manipulative spirit. He would yell at us and then be nice to us two seconds later. It was a rollercoaster ride with how he treated us. He didn't act like this initially, because he needed me to train him. After he got hired, the front desk director hired an overnight supervisor, Tisha, instead of giving the position to me. I kind of didn't expect them to give it to me. I figured that they would have given it to me by now if they wanted me to have it. Tisha was a short lady who was soft-spoken who also walked with a slight limp. She was about fifty-four years old but looked like she could easily pass for forty-five. I mean this lady was in shape, with a young face. She was pretty with a nice personality. I trained them all on their roles including supported them in their positions.

I had many responsibilities. I would take a break by parking in a public parking lot to sleep in my car for about thirty minutes. Before my class, I would drive to a diner in Madison where they cooked the best waffles and veggie omelet. While I would be sitting there, two different men said that my eyes sparkled. One of them asked if I knew that my eyes would sparkle and of course I didn't. I would go home to look in the mirror examine my eyes wondering if I could see what those two men saw. I never did.

At my place, I began to exercise in my room. Whenever I exercised listening to music, I would break out dancing. I remember hearing the Holy Spirit tell me to watch how I was dancing. I couldn't figure out why He said that when I was in the privacy of my room with the door shut. I wasn't doing anything crazy inappropriate, but I would drop it like it's hot as if I was in somebody's music video. Since I worked the overnight shift, I rarely saw my two roommates. They worked during the day, although I did hear the cab driver coming home to use the bathroom like every other hour. I thought that was out of the ordinary.

Sometimes the other roommate the painter would travel to Columbia for a couple of months and return back to work per his normal schedule. This time around, he went to Columbia for about two months and returned with a woman named Rosa. The landlord said that all the years that he had lived there, this was the first time he had ever brought a woman home. She had never seen him with a woman and she knew him for about ten years.

Rosa was cool. She only spoke Spanish so she needed help finding a job. I invited her to my room to sit down to help her look for work online. Once we established what she was suited for, I drove her to the library so that she could apply. She called me a saint. When we got back to the house, she was also gaining trust with the landlord. She was over in the kitchen cooking food and I could hear them laughing and talking as if they were old friends. A few days later I could see Rosa leaving the painters bedroom with dishes in her hand. Next thing I know is that I could hear her washing those same dishes in our bathroom. I opened my bedroom door to see Rosa bent over the bathtub washing dishes. This was the most ludicrous way of cleaning dishes I ever saw in my life. I hurried out of my bedroom to ask her to please use the kitchen instead of the bathroom tub and sink. Rosa didn't understand a word that came out of my mouth. I pulled out my chrome book to use the translator. She seemed to understand once I walked away because she did stop. I could hear her cooking in the kitchen so I thought maybe I would help with this problem. I went out and purchased them some plastic plates and silverware. However, on my days off from work, I could hear Rosa washing their dishes yet again in our shared bathtub. I was sent over the edge. I went to the bathroom to talk to her once again. We began to argue loudly that the landlord left her side of the house to come and intervene. Rosa was screaming at me like a lunatic. To my surprise, the landlord sided with Rosa and said that it was okay for her to wash the dishes in our bathroom. No one took my feelings into consideration or how I could see this as being sickening. I left notes in the bathroom both in English and Spanish that read, please use the kitchen, Por favor, deje de lavar los platos en la banera y el lavabo. Por favor usa la cocina. Gracias

I went to work and spent the night at my job due to a few snowstorms. New Jersey had a blackout which caused a chaos. People were in the line running out of gas while standing in line for gas because the gas stations ran out of gas to give to the people. It was horrible and New Jersey was not ready for it. When I heard through the news that people were spending the night on the train and shopping centers because of the storm I left my car at home to take the bus to and from work. I spent the night for about four days at work. When I got home, the landlord told me as soon as I walked through the door that Rosa was kicked out. According to the landlord, she and Rosa got into a heated argument. The painter went back to Columbia and left Rosa at the house. The landlord didn't tell me what they argued about. All I know was that Rosa told her that she was not leaving because she was a tenant. The Landlord threatened to take the door off the hinges to kick her out since the painter was only paying for him to stay there and not for Rosa to live there too. I'm thankful to return to a stress-free environment.

I was preparing to meet the gospel singer Erica Campbell at my job. I was ecstatic when I heard that she was coming into town and would be staying at my establishment. For the past few weeks, I had been communicating with a young lady who was the daughter of a pastor where Erica would be visiting to perform at her father's birthday celebration. I talked with the daughter just making sure that her company was set up and that Erica had a gift upon her arrival. All the years working at my job, I never got to see the several Christian and Gospel artist that came through. I usually got into work too late but this time Erica would be arriving during my Overnight shift. My excitement almost overshadowed the fact that I wrote a rather interesting comment on her Facebook post when she released her first solo song. I wrote that I needed a little more Tina to replace her lyrics that she needed a little more Jesus. I never knew that Erica was bothered by my comment until I went on YouTube on my lunch break. I saw an interview where the interviewer asked Tina and Erica how their fans reacted to them going solo. When Erica Campbell responded by mentioning my comment I was anxious. I didn't know that it bothered her to the point that it stuck with her. Her visiting my work establishment would be a way for me to make amends.

The night that Erica was arriving at my job her assistant called me from their car to ask about a place to eat, so I directed them to the nearest 24-hour diner. After they finished eating, Erica and her team were right in front of me. I wore my straight hair wig instead of my normal curly one. For the first time ever, the daughter of the pastor asked me if I wanted to meet Erica. Never had a celebrity assistant asked me to meet them, but the daughter of the pastor said that I was so helpful that if I wanted to meet her, I could. Oh my goodness, I had to keep my composure since I was a huge Mary Mary fan. She was beautiful and such a delight. When they led her to me, she looked at me as if she recognized me. I just smiled as we shook hands, but I had nothing to say. I could see her trying to look at my name tag that was somewhat hidden by my long straight hair but I could tell that she figured it out. I just gave her this awkward smile and said nothing to the effect because I'm at work. What am I really supposed to say while my boss standing there?

A week later, Michelle Williams came into my establishment. She stood in front of my boss who helped assist her. I walked over to Michelle Williams to shake her hands as she was even more gorgeous in person. Her makeup, hair, and the dress was flawless. Her pictures don't do her justice in my opinion. But I perceived in my spirit that she knew about the Erica and our situation at least that's what I believe. When I went to shake her hands, she shook it but gave me that look like she's team Erica.

Later that night, I met Patti LaBelle. I was beyond mesmerized that she was standing in front of me. I asked Patti LaBelle if I could shake her hands. She looked at me and came around to me to give me a hug. Patti Labelle gave me a hug, and then she danced with her past Dancing with the Stars partner right in front of me. Talk about lighting up my life. I never thought in a million years to ever meet a top celebrity neither that person giving me a hug. Thanks, Patti LaBelle. You are a true light. Thanks for being used by Jesus.

The next day one member of my church family asked me, along with a couple of other ladies, if we wanted to go to Pennsylvania for the weekend to see Joyce Meyer and Israel Houghton and New Breed minister. It was a dream to see Joyce Meyer and Israel Houghton. I had looked up to them both, along with many incredible artists who God has used to spread His word. God was sending me to places and meet all these incredible men and women of God. I felt like God was setting me up for success. I decided at the last minute that I wanted to come. We drove to Pennsylvania listening to gospel music. I had enough money to purchase a pink Joyce Meyer T-shirt. Man, the Joyce Meyer conference was impeccable beyond my imagination. Just what God ordered for my soul and body. She preached three times and I got to see and hear her those three days. We got up in the morning and ate a free breakfast. During the breaks of the Joyce Meyer conference, I separated myself to walk to a nearby park, sit in silence, and take it all in. I was inhaling gratefulness.

The second round of Joyce Meyer and Israel and New Breed, we danced like we never praised before. I was all over the place on the bottom dance floor. I surely represented a worshipper. God had been good to me and it was my time to shout in praise and worship. They kept me on my feet.

I Am Fearfully and Wonderfully Made

This year, 2015 I reminisced about all of my blessings. Through the ups and downs and several challenges, God has kept me alive, healthy, and safe. I've endured many trials and tribulation but I have overcome them all. God has been my rock and inspiration! My source of strength in the days of trouble. I received a phone call from Olivia asking me if I wanted to come back to Florida to be with her two daughters while she went with her husband to see his family in another country. Immediately I planned my trip. I was down in Florida before you knew it. When I arrived Olivia was whispering in her daughter's ears. Olivia told me that the girls had their own credit card which they both had a budget and that the oldest could drive the car. I didn't know what their budget was which was odd to me. This trip would be nothing like when I visited them when they lived with their father.

I had a full week of fun things planned while their mother and stepfather were in another country. The first couple of nights I wanted us girls to bond. We went shopping at the grocery store to prepare a hearty meal. As soon as we entered the grocery store the girls disappeared on me. They sort of left me alone instead of shopping with me. The next day the girls and I drove to Orlando to go to the Holy Land Experience. We spent the entire day out there. The girls were good sports in letting me enjoy a day of "bible" experiences. After the park, Olivia's oldest daughter got in the driver seat to drive to the hotel to rest for the night and then we were to head to Disney the following morning.

We stopped for gas, which I let her pump. As she was driving to the hotel, the car immediately began to make noises and jerk like it was turning off. Good thing that it didn't turn off until we got off the highway, about a five-minute drive from the hotel. I had to help drive while I sat on the passenger side because the wheel was locking up. We managed to pull into a driveway, but the car turned off as soon as we turned. I had no idea what was the matter with my friend's car. Her car should not be stopping. I called their father in a panic about what to do next. Their father calmed me down and assured us that all would be okay. The girls finally got a hold of their mom who called a tow truck. We were towed to a local P&P. The P&P had us scheduled to look at the car the following morning since they were closed for business when we arrived. The girls and I had a good night's rest at the hotel with me sleeping on the couch and they share the bed. The following morning while at P&P we found out that Olivia's daughter pumped diesel instead of regular gas. Olivia had to pay hundreds of dollars to get her car fixed while she was vacationing out of country. She was yelling and screaming at all of us. There went our plans. Disney was no longer an option. I had to drive us back four hours to their house. We stayed in the house for the rest of the week, except the last night, when I suggested that we go bowling. I felt like it was an honest mistake and this was also my vacation trip. After we went bowling we drove to Miami to get a little more fun in before I left. It's one of my favorite parts of my trip while visiting Florida to walk on the strip, listening to music while we're eating and drinking a refreshing beverage.

Olivia was not happy with me and blamed the entire experience on me. At the airport, I received a phone call from Olivia's ex-husband, asking me if I knew about a check that was written by his daughter. Olivia's oldest daughter gave her account number to some friends, who stole some money from the bank account she shared with her dad. Now that made sense why all this disaster happened in Orlando. Maybe God prevented the fun from happening because Olivia's daughter allowed her friends to steal underneath my nose. That was one wild trip to say it mildly.

Too bad that when I returned home, my Buick began to stop on me every other month. I was paying more in getting it fixed than I should. My mechanic would fix it, but then my car would break down again in the middle of the street. It was embarrassing. It was time for me to give up Betsy and find a new car. I could no longer afford to keep up this car maintenance, and it was happening way too often. I even had taken my car to another mechanic and still, the car would start running and then all of a sudden my tires would get on a flat. I even purchased another tire and still, I got another flat on the same tire that I replaced. It was a sign for me to let this car go and get a reliable one.

That night I came out to my car to see that someone placed a postcard on my windshield saying that they would tow and pay me. I needed the money and I needed this car towed. Before I did this, I called to apply to get financed for a new car. I didn't get approved for the amount of money that I wanted, but it was enough where the bank referred me to a smaller dealership. I called them because I needed a car in a hurry. I told the salesman, who happened to be the owner, that I needed a car ASAP. I only had $500 for a down payment, but I needed a car because I had an overnight job and I went to school. I needed reliable transportation. The salesman described the car that he wanted to sell to me over the telephone which sounded good to me. I just needed to see it but I did trust this salesman as I explained several times my need for reliable transportation.

But when I got to his lot, he had a white Chevrolet Blazer in front of me instead of the one that he had described to me over the telephone. One of my church member friends dropped me off at the dealership at night. I inspected the SUV. On the outside, it looked fine, with the exception of a crack on the windshield, which the owner said he would replace. Everything else to the eye seemed okay. I filled out the paperwork with the promise that this SUV was in good working condition. I gave him the $500 and he drove me in the Chevrolet Blazer to a gas station to get gas, since this Blazer was on empty. As the gas attendant was pumping the gas, the pump kept stopping. I looked back as I could hear the pump stop. The owner stepped out of the SUV, and when I asked him what the matter was, he said that the gas station pump had problems.

I drove my new used SUV off the lot blasting my music feeling really good about myself. Now the tank was not full, not even close. The very next morning the SUV wouldn't start. When it finally cranked up, I drove it to the gas station to get more gas, but the pump was doing the same thing that it did the night before when the owner said that the pump had a problem. Now I was at a different gas station with the same problem. It was not the gas stations pump something was wrong with this SUV not being able to receive gas fully. The gas attendant eventually had to stop pumping the gas because the gas was backing out and leaking onto the car and onto the gas attendant's hands. I called the owner of the used car lot where I got this SUV while I was at work. He assured me that it was a simple fix. He would get the windshield replaced, replace the battery and find the parts for the gas. He made good on his promise with all that I mentioned except finding the parts for my gas. He kept giving me the runaround. He would tell me that he had the part then I would drive nearly forty minutes away to his car lot to drive off with the same problem. I couldn't even drive this SUV under these conditions. I must've driven to this salesman car lot five times before I broke down in tears and called the police to report a scam going on. The police couldn't do much for me. I ended up leaving that SUV in that salesman parking lot, called a cab to come and pick me up which I had to pay over $100. I was livid. Now I had no car because I got my Buick towed, and I had no SUV. I had to take the train and bus to and from work, which was a nightmare on Elm Street.

I had to take the train at 10:30 pm to Madison, then wait for a bus that came about fifteen minutes later, and it was dusty and filthy. I sat with my feet up in the air because there was so much trash on the bus floor. In the morning, when I got off of work at 7:30 am if I didn't run across the street to take the 7:45 am the bus, I had to wait until 10 am for the next bus to go home. I think I caught the 7:45 am bus like twice. All the other times, I had to wait in the mall for the 10 am. I didn't get home many times until noon. It was the dead of winter, so it was cold and raining and since I was just learning the bus schedule, I missed the bus and had to call a cab to pick me up. Multiple times I was late to come in for work because I didn't know that the bus location for pickup had changed because they didn't advertise the change. It wasn't posted online or anywhere. My bosses were not showing compassion towards me. You would think since I had been working for the company for five years that I would receive a little sympathy, yet they gave me none. I was trying my best. Many times I went home frustrated and in tears for all that I had to endure. It was rough taking public transportation all while working an Overnight schedule.

I rode the public transportation for about three weeks when I felt confident that I had mastered this transportation system. I knew what time to get up for work so that I could make it on time for the train. I was taking the cab sometimes to work, which was costly, but at least it gave my body and mind a break. I knew what time the bus came to pick me up. In the morning I began to bring a Chromebook to the mall while I sat down to wait for the bus to take me home. I had a routine down pat.

I woke up to a cold night as I prepared to get my night started. I layered up in clothes. I had a pair of jogging paints underneath my work pants, two pairs of socks, my work shirt with a hoodie, plus my winter coat. I headed out of the house to walk down the street to catch the train. The traffic light signaled for me to cross the crosswalk when I looked to my right to make sure it was safe for me to walk across. In the middle of the crosswalk, I was struck by a truck. My head and right side of my body hit the truck hard and then I fell to the cold ground. I could only lift up my head. I tried to move my body, but I lost all movement from my chest down. My legs lost all movement. I was on the cold ground with my eyes to the ground when all I wanted to do was get up and get to work. I could hear people surrounding me telling me not to get up, especially a man kept saying, "Don't try to move," but I couldn't move. I was conscious but I couldn't get up, even when I tried. I couldn't even try.

The policeman instructed me to not move. I told them that I had to go to work. The police told me that I wasn't going to work that night. Then the ambulance came and placed me on a stretcher. The police bent down to tell me that he would meet me at the hospital. I said okay. The ambulance tried to adjust me that's when I could feel my wig pulling back, now that was a problem since I had lost some of my edges. Some of my feeling in my arm was coming back so I used all of my strength to adjust my wig and bring it back to the front. I got in the ambulance truck, and they ripped my pants. I called my boss to try to explain what just happened to me when an EMT grabbed my cell phone out of my hand to explain what happened to my boss. He told them that I was not going to make it to work. When I arrived at the hospital, they placed me in a room by myself.

The straps that were wrapped around my body while lying on the stretcher caused me to panic. I felt like I couldn't breath and my blood pressure was high due to this. One of the nurses kept coming in and out of my room. I begged her to please loosen the straps but she wouldn't. I regained feeling in my body, although I was sore, so I began to try to loosen it myself. The nurse told me that I needed to stay strapped up so the doctor could examine me to see if I had any broken bones or fractures. I told the nurse that I had neither and I needed her to loosen me, but she refused. When she left, I managed to loosen the straps myself and lie down comfortably. I laid my hands on my body and declared that God had healed me and there were no broken bones and that I was healed in the name of Jesus.

The doctor came into my room because the nurse told her that I loosed myself. The doctor examined me and sent me to get X-rays. The doctor had a great report for me. She said that I did not have one broken bone. I was sore, and limping on my right side. I had a knot on my head with scratches on my shoulder, head, and hand. But I was good to go home that night. The police came to visit me when he felt that I was in good shape to talk. He began to tell me that I must've gotten hit pretty hard because I was far away from the crosswalk. He said that the driver's truck got towed. The driver lied and said that he tried to stop for me, but when the police examined the tires of the truck, they saw this was a lie and there were no signs of that on the road. Also, this guy was driving someone else's truck, with no driver's license. The police officer was polite and spoke with care like he was concerned for my well-being. I called a cab to pick me up to take me home.

This accident happened around the holiday. I already had days requested off, so I only had to return to work for a couple of days, then I stayed home for about a week. I was sore, but I was all in one piece. I wasn't paralyzed, although people told me to go see a specialist. I had already claimed my healing so there was no need. God healed me. God said by his stripes I am healed, I am fearfully and wonderfully made.

CPSIA information can be obtained
at www.ICGtesting.com
Printed in the USA
BVHW041149260719
554453BV00007B/59/P

9 781545 669556